The Anxiety
of
Interdisciplinarity

de-, dis-, ex-.

Volume Two

Edited by: ALEX COLES and ALEXIA DEFERT

Distributed by Art Books International Ltd, 1 Stewart's Court, 220 Stewart's
Road, London SW8 4UD, UK.
Tel: 0171 720 1530   Fax: 0171 720 3158

Published by BACKless Books in association with Black Dog Publishing
de-, dis-, ex-. © 1998

ISBN 1 901033 75 9

Set in Caecilia and Frutiger

de-, dis-, ex-.

de-, dis-, ex

Volume Two

The Anxiety of Interdisciplinarity

Contributors:

Howard Caygill is Professor of Cultural History at Goldsmiths College, University of London. He is the author of *Art of Judgment* (1989), *A Kant Dictionary* (1995), and *Walter Benjamin: The Colour of Experience* (1997).

Alex Coles is founding editor of *de-, dis-, ex-.* and co-author of *Walter Benjamin for Beginners*. He is currently undertaking Phd research at Goldsmiths' College where he is also a visiting lecturer.

Beatriz Colomina is Assistant Professor in the Department of Architecture at Princeton University. She is the editor of *Sexuality and Space* and the author of *Privacy and Publicity: Modern Architecture as Mass Publicity.*

Alexia Defert is a freelance editor and visiting lecturer at various colleges across London. She is currently undertaking Phd research at the Slade School of Fine Art, University College of London.

Hal Foster is Professor of Modern Art at Princeton University. He is a co-editor of the journal *October* and most recently author of *The Return of the Real* (MIT Press).

Candida Höfer is an artist who lives and works in Cologne. Since 1979 she has been photographing communal rooms in public buildings across Europe.

Rosalind Krauss is Meyer Schapiro Professor of Modern Art at Columbia University. She is a founding editor of the journal *October*.

Julia Kristeva is a psychoanalyst and Professor of Linguistics at University Paris VII. She is the author of many books, including *Powers of Horror*, *Strangers to Ourselves* and *Proust and the Sense of Time* (all Columbia University Press).

Louis Martin is currently undertaking Phd research at Princeton University. His articles have appeared in *Parachute*, *assemblage*, and ARQ.

Timothy Martin is currently a visiting lecturer in the History of Art Department, University of Reading. His reviews and articles have appeared in *Art History*, *Third Text*, *Frieze* and *Art Monthly*.

Introduction

Just *Who* is Anxious?

> You see, Jacques, when you leave your own realm,
> when you attempt to be consistent, whatever that
> might mean in architecture, it is precisely then that
> you do not understand the implications for decon-
> struction in architecture - when deconstruction leaves
> your hands.

The publication of the Eisenman/Derrida letters in *assemblage* 12
(1990) following Derrida's carefully orchestrated withdrawal from a
conference on postmodernism and architecture, drove home a
timely point in a succinct but callous manner. By expressing their
unease with each other's involvement in their joint project, the
Chora work, both parties disclosed their *anxiety*. The anxiety was
alleviated, however, not by being critically worked through, but
rather by being sublimated: Eisenman and Derrida returned to their
respective fields.

Cast in terms of the mood of this deadlock, the present volume
intervenes in the debates both on the history and future of interdisciplinary exchanges between art, architecture and theory - and their
practice, criticism and historicisation - by offering a series of broad
yet focused insights. The principle organising the volume is a commitment towards assembling critical interdisciplinary trajectories.
On the one hand, this entails resisting the motivation of tropes such

de-, dis-, ex-.

as 'translation' (too often an alibi for avoiding critical interdisciplinary work), and on the other, repressing the regressive desire to return to the pragmatic demands of a discipline.

In entirely different ways, focusing the trajectory of the volume are the optics of two periods of vigorous interdisciplinary work: the late-1960s-early-1970s and the mid-1990s to the present. For while Julia Kristeva reflects on the genealogy of her interdisciplinary journey from the 1960s onwards, Timothy Martin's essay on Robert Smithson reflects on a practitioner from this period so as to reassess his relevance to the present. By interpreting Smithson's writings in correspondence with an underprivileged art work, Martin adjusts the way Smithson is often subordinated to exterior theoretical paradigms. In the same way, while Rosalind Krauss' overlooked text on Peter Eisenman from 1977 self-reflectively charts her journey from formalism in the 1960s to postmodernism through looking across at a parallel architectural practice, Louis Martin chronicles the interdisciplinary trajectory of Bernard Tschumi by interpreting Tschumi's intertextual theoretical work begun in the early 1970s in correspondence with his architectural practice. In contrast to these methodological approaches, Beatriz Colomina excavates an as yet untheorised architectural practice. Her methodology of surfacing the full spectrum of the Eames output clarifies the ways new media activated previously unmotivated sites for the architectural practitioner. In this way Colomina extends her commitment of assessing the interdisciplinary role the media plays in architectural production.

Symptomatic of the *anxiety of interdisciplinarity* is a return to outmoded paradigms of judgement. While in view of Hal Foster's and Julia Kristeva's conversations it is clear that judgement is still an important criteria for assessing the legitimacy of new interdisciplinary configurations, their respective practice of judgement transforms its very lineaments. Kristeva and Foster reflect on their interdisciplinary methodologies; with both affirming that "to be interdisciplinary you need to be disciplinary first - to be grounded in one discipline, preferably two, to know historically of these discourses before you test them against each other."

Two commissioned projects offer further possibilities - especially when considered in correspondence to each other. While Candida Höfer establishes a photographic survey of the institutional interiors of both old and new sites of academic practice, Howard Caygill outmodes them in a move that reconfigures the parameters of what an interdisciplinary field can constitute, namely, by immersing philosophy in an urban experience focused through the lens of a throw-away camera.

With a heterogeneity of critical methodologies, this volume documents the obligation for working through the *anxiety of interdisciplinarity*. As most of these contributions confess it is only by maintaining the degree of uncertainty that interdisciplinary work bears - while simultaneously producing critiques of earlier sites of interdisciplinary practice - that new sites can be progressively opened up.

Alex Coles and

Alexia Defert

London, Spring 1998

de-, dis-, ex-.

Julia Kristeva

Institutional Interdisciplinarity in Theory and in Practice

An interview

Politics of Interdisciplinarity

Alexia Defert: Looking at the totality of your work as well as back issues of Tel Quel, it becomes clear that your commitment to interdisciplinarity goes back a long way. The first thing I would like to know is what the word connotes to you, both in relation to your own trajectory and with regard to current projects?

Julia Kristeva: The word connotes many different things. As it happens, my own education as well as possibly my personal inclinations seemed to predispose me to work in an interdisciplinary manner. From a very young age, I was interested in sciences, and my real ambition was actually to study nuclear physics or astronomy. Yet in Bulgaria at the time, as my parents did not belong to the Communist party, it was impossible for me to go and study in the appropriate schools in Russia. Thus I had to abandon the project, but I have always kept an interest in the pure sciences. I then decided I wanted to study medicine, which in itself is also a rather technical and precise science, but as there too the School of Medicine was not open to me, still for the same political reasons, I ended up studying the humanities! I studied with great passion, concentrating on French literature, then English Literature, and in the end received a degree in comparative literature. There I discovered that - as Mallarmé says - literature is at the crossroads of all the other disciplines. This may sound a little bit eclectic, but all in all, no other discipline seems to point to the polyvalence of the human mind the way literature does. Far from being a backdrop or a decorum, literature is, as I find myself saying more and more, the very process of thinking caught in its unfolding. Nowhere but in literature, and I am thinking here of the classics, can one be exposed to and at the same time grasp the progression of thought, in this most radical manner. What is at stake here is the possibility of witnessing a thinking-process, far away from a calculating mode of thinking, a robotic thinking-process, laid out only to solve a problem according to a binary logic. Through studying literature, I explored many routes such as philology, the history of ideas, the biographies of authors, their psychology and so on, which led me to be more and more interested in the complexities of the creative experience. At that time my own trajectory happened to be crossing the path of a movement which, in the light of recent critical trends, appears a slightly reductive and positivist project, but which still has much to offer: Structuralism.

In the 60s, Structuralism reflected a real desire to understand the creative experience, yet through an interpretative grid that could be mastered. In other words, one was concerned with abandoning the cowardice and the evasiveness of ongoing discourses such as impressionist psychology on the one hand, or else sociology, which would seem an incredibly reductive discourse, in the way it would submit the creative experience to social or biographical determinations, emphasising class-struggle and production, without attempting to understand the logic of symbolic creativity itself. This logic seemed inevitably linked to the logic of language: whether one is a musician, an architect, a painter or a writer, we are all trying to signify something. Thus the logic of language appeared to be the primordial symbolic material available from which to start in order to understand other signifying practices.

AD: *This approach has historical precedents but how did you arrive at psychoanalysis?*

JK: Yes, its historical precedents corresponded to the Russian Formalists' approach, further developed by Structuralism. It is in that continuity that I started working upon my arrival in Paris, having myself studied linguistics and discovered Russian Formalism through my studies in Bulgaria. But with regard to my own work, I soon realised both the benefits and the limitations of Structuralism. My task then was to overtake these limits, which I would characterise as being twofold: on the one hand, Structuralism does not take into account creative subjectivity, that is, ignores the question of the subject; and, on the other hand, it bypasses the historical context in which work is being produced. These two flaws were to orientate me, beside my interest in linguistics, towards two, if not more, new disciplines: as far as the subject is concerned, psychoanalysis, and as far as the reevaluation of historical and social frameworks are concerned, history, sociology and, more generally, philosophy. My first encounter with interdisciplinarity starts there, with the clear necessity to work disciplines differently but in parallel.

AD: *Was the term 'interdisciplinarity' in use at that time?*

JK: The word in itself perhaps not, but clearly, in that same period of time, the necessity to access all human experiences from different angles started to find a name for itself, to be 'topicalised', for instance, in France, by the notion of 'polyvalence'. In this first phase, interdisciplinarity was a site of great enthusiasm but after a while we started to realise that as a site of encounter amongst various forms of practices, it constituted a very difficult, if not perilous, enterprise.

AD: *Could you say a bit more on these difficulties, if not dangers, as they were emerging?*

de-, dis-, ex-.

JK: Interdisciplinarity is always a site where expressions of resistance are latent. Many academics are locked within the specificity of their field; that is a fact. Even if they demonstrate or manifest a desire to work with other disciplines, more often than not it turns out that, in fact, the work undertaken fails to break new ground. Thus, the first obstacle is often linked to individual competences coupled with a tendency to jealously protect one's own domain. Specialists are often too protective of their own prerogatives, do not actually work with other colleagues, and therefore do not teach their students to construct a diagonal axis in their methodology. As for dangerous aspects, you will find that some people think their specialisation is interdisciplinarity itself, which is tantamount to saying that they have a limited amount of knowledge of various domains, and only fragmentary competences! This gives interdisciplinarity a very caricatural image, and altogether reduces its scope as a project.

Here at University Paris VII, the whole college has an interdisciplinary vocation. We do try to promote its practise, yet very often when we have meetings and analyse the results, we have to measure the difficulties inherent in the nature of such an enterprise. One cannot be an amateur, or decide one day 'Let's be interdisciplinary'. A university may decide to develop in that direction, but what matters is that each researcher finds and establishes some complicities with other researchers so that interdisciplinarity comes from the base of the pyramid and works its way up. In other words, it is not simply a matter of the good will of the French educational authorities. One can only benefit from interdisciplinary practices if researchers meet other researchers whilst learning how to discuss both their competences and the outcome of their interaction; therefore contributing to the exposure of the risks inherent in an interdisciplinary practice. But what I am suggesting here is specific to the difficulties of this university and we are all very much aware of the necessity to underline them. But there are some good points too. For instance, at Paris VII, we have founded *L' Institut du Vivant* (*The Institute of the Living*). The idea here is to approach the human being in its complexities across the disciplines. This mobilises linguists, semioticians such as myself, but also academics from the literature department who are interested in the thinking-practice constituted by literature, as well as psychoanalysts who are posing questions regarding the logic of creativity in relation to the difficulties of human experience. We also work with biologists, since, after all, life is their prime domain, as well as historians, sociologists and lawyers too (the moment you are discussing, for instance, questions of artificial procreation legal questions inevitably arise). I think this institute is one of the few of its kind in the world. Equally, we offer a diploma for researchers in psychology and semiology that attracts psychology students, as well as doctors and linguists. Thus we are trying to give an official existence to these practices through the granting of degrees, so that it does not just remain an individual experience. At that level, the principal difficulty encountered comes from the fact that previous studies have often equipped students with capacities which can reveal themselves insufficient for the other field. Thus, even with a real desire on the student's part to master these different disciplines, it remains a difficult path of studies, one, it has to be said, that requires more work than usual courses do.

AD: *While we are discussing the particularities of this university, I would like to know whether the question of theory and practice, and the old anxiety of seeing one prioritised over the other, arises? For instance, what does one arrive at, working in literature across psychoanalysis and linguistics, if*

de-, dis-, ex-.

not a 'supra-theory'?

JK: There is of course a danger of seeing practice disappear. I may surprise you here, but I would like to say how much I personally value a 'hands-on experience', a concrete experience of literature for instance. When I say this might surprise you, I am partly referring to the fact that I am mainly read as a theoretician, whose abstract theories should rise well above a general state of confusion...but, in fact, this could not be farther from both my personal experience and from my intentions. I have always attempted to combine theory with concrete and practical experience. Obviously, this presupposes both a great facility for abstract thought and a capacity to give oneself over to one's own experience. For instance, a student in literature or in architecture needs to have a basic knowledge of Freud, Hegel or Heidegger, and needs to know a bit of linguistic theory; inevitably, this is going to happen outside his or her 'time of practice'. But the danger consists in locking oneself up in these theories and losing the connection with the demands and logic inherent in one's own practice. This is where the person in charge of the theoretical side or the person in charge of the studio-practice needs to intervene to equip the student with the means to maintain a dynamic diagonal axis between both poles. I very often see students who are enthusiastic readers of theory such as Freud's or Heidegger's. Although they may end up with brilliant *exposés*, when it comes to their reading of Proust, they can't always locate the link between Freud or Heidegger and Proust. Consequently, I ask them to momentarily set aside their fetishism of Freud or Heidegger in favour of their experience of reading Proust. Theoretical research is important but it remains a preparatory work which is insufficient if not tested by concrete experience. One thing is made clear to students: we will not become philosophers in the literature department nor will we become psychoanalysts within the time of the course. Our work is to ensure that the infusion of this high theory into the material - which constitutes the starting point of the enquiry - is seen through. The prime material must always be returned to; it must not be forgotten in favour of theory; on the contrary, it must be enriched and explained in an unprecedented manner in order to take the theoretical text somewhere new. For instance, if a literature student is supposed to suggest a new reading of a text by Proust, the aim of the exercise is partly to bring the student to write, to become a writer, with a different input, a different angle on Proust, informed both by his or her reading of theoretical texts, but rooted in his or her experience of Proust. I personally value concrete experience. There is thus for me no real resolving of the old practice/theory debate but the dialectic is enriching.

AD: In relation to this balancing exercise you are describing, I would like to focus on the concept of abjection. From the 60s onwards, your work has been dedicated to the surfacing of new readings of both classics and modern avant-garde works of literature, borrowing from varied disciplines, such as semiotics, philosophy and psychoanalysis. Yet with Powers of Horror (1980), one senses a shift in the coming together of a theory, whereby the concept of abjection seems to impose itself on you, through your experience of Céline's writing. Could you come back to this encounter with Céline's writing and retrace the genealogy of the concept of abjection whose scope reaches well beyond that of an 'aesthetic theory'?

JK: To start with, it had nothing to do with an aesthetic theory. My reading of Céline originated in my experience as an analyst which, as always, is rooted in one's own personal experience. At the time, I was working on Céline because he is an extremely complicated author, both fascinating as an artist, and yet problematic because of

de-, dis-, ex-.

his ideology. Thus, I started studying his texts with my students in a very empirical manner in order for them to familiarise themselves with *Journey to the End of the Night, Death on the Instalment Plan* as well as with the antisemitic pamphlets. Then I started to wonder how I might synthesise all this work, that is, not just synthesise the texts but bring a different interpretative reading of the texts. Parallel to this, I was pursuing my work as an analyst. There, I was confronted with violent experiences, experiences of rejection, decay, encounters with horror, all this both at the level of phobia and at the level of psychosis. It is whilst working in this double register, a little bit as would the conductor of an orchestra working with several instruments, that a melody took shape. And I very clearly remember this particular moment where I was lying in bed at night and when the word 'abjection' came to me, at the crossroads between different thoughts. I insist a little bit deliberately on this rather nocturnal and dreamlike situation for these situations are made possible by the fact that, at night, our conscious filters are weaker; that is, our intellectual mechanisms are at work, but by way of analogies rather than by obedience to the rigorous mastering of concepts. Thus the whole thinking-process itself becomes closer to an aesthetic process, and this is how the term 'abjection' came to the fore of my mind. In that same moment, I also suddenly measured how much the word seemed to crystallise Céline's personal experience, his style as well as the way he had compromised himself politically. All I had to do then was to back it up, to develop it in psychoanalytical terms, in social terms as well as in philosophical and political terms. But the starting point occurred in this dreamlike state that I have described.

AD: Do you think that such a concept could have been arrived at, might have been formulated, without your experience as an analyst and the para-

meters this provided you with?

JK: Possibly not this concept, but psychoanalysis is not compulsory for this kind of work. It turned out that in my experience it was necessary and it constituted in some ways the strongest element. Let me briefly tell you why. When you are in the process of analysis your practice consists of listening to others, you are receiving their problems, you are asking them questions about themselves; but at the same time you find yourself very strongly implicated. Arriving at the notion of abjection would have been probably impossible without my personal implication. In many ways, through identifying with the patient's distress, I become the patient. My practice as an analyst always connects me to the distress of others, sometimes dealing with more or less serious forms of distress, but as I invest in these situations, they become almost fictional. Thus, the process becomes close to the experience of writing a novel: I experience the same level of implication. It is this very level of implication that I find primordial in order, as a theoretician, to remain creative, to not reiterate other peoples theories but to modify them, to ensure a transformation. The worst that can happen with students, and sometimes it has happened with colleagues abroad, is for them to appropriate a notion and apply it in a dogmatic way. It's probably inevitable, but sometimes it is excessive and then mostly counter-productive for the person engaged in that process. I'd rather my own approach constituted a starting point from which to develop, from which to work away, and if it is to be in an unfaithful manner, so be it, as long as the reader's own creativity and inventiveness are stimulated.

AD: I am interested in these ideas of appropriation and unfaithfulness. The notion of abjection has certainly stimulated the minds of many critics and

de-, dis-, ex-.

curators from the mid-80s onwards, I am thinking for instance of the Abject Art exhibition which took place at the Whitney Museum of American Art in 1993 and which directly refers to Powers of Horror. What do you think of such an appropriation?

JK: Unfortunately, I did not get to see the show but I was told about it, so it would be difficult for me to comment. I do think that the notion of abjection suits certain forms of artistic practices in a very authentic manner, but in other ways it is rather superimposed onto the work and it becomes too literal. But I cannot generalise....

Visions of America

AD: In 1977, Tel Quel published a double issue on America (Tel Quel 71: 'Pourquoi les Etats-Unis?').

In this double issue, compiled after an extended visit to America, you described in a conversation with Marcelin Pleynet and Philippe Sollers, your interest in the 'grafting principle', specific, according to you, to the American culture. In this discussion, you describe the possibility in America to "enter multiple discourses at once," in relation to a social porosity and forms of cultural exchanges amongst a variety of social groups which you thought at the time impossible to envisage in Europe. In this overall account of your experience of America, two aspects interest me in the light of today's discussion. One is a sense that artistic practices were, in the 70s, much more visible in America, and the second is your description of a 'polyvalence', as if multiculturalism had had the effect of contributing towards the undoing of disciplininary traditions inherited from the old continent. Is there, do you think, still such a difference between Europe and America, in their respective practise of interdisciplinarity?

JK: Two things had struck me at the time. One was the decentralised aspect of American society, which compared to France and its roaring Jacobinism seemed to open up forms of discussion susceptible of having repercussions on debates concerning the modernisation of French society. The second aspect that struck me was the way in which artistic practices - bearing in mind this goes back twenty or twenty-five years - seemed to constitute a site of curiosity for a part of the population not necessarily versed in art and its contemporary forms, but which seemed to access the art scene by entering into communion with a kind of secular form of the sacred. One could argue here that since traditional American art does not exist as such, the absence of an ancient cultural past combined with an intense search for religiosity, led a new part of American society to seek access to contemporary art-forms in the 70s. That thirst for religious experiences seemed suddenly quenched by aesthetic experiences. In relation to this, Europe adopted a more clear-headed position. And it is here, in this desire to understand and rationalise experience, that you find the roots of a cultural emphasis on theory. Since the early 70s, obviously, the graft of European theories operated onto American culture has taken: it manifests itself in the form of an interdisciplinarity. It arises through the importance given to French theory as well as German theory, the Frankfurt School, Structuralism, Post-Structuralism, Deconstruction and the appropriation of my own work too. Thus artists have read and learnt to theorise, which, in return, has changed the face of practise. Artists are still pursuing their experience as practitioners, but in a less naive manner, accompanying their formal development with a reflection. Yet that is not to say that the sacred aspect has been lost altogether. Having visited America many times since, especially in recent years, it is my impression that this intensity, this cultural renewal, which characterises the American art scene of the 70s, has settled in a more commercial credo: there is thus a kind of complacency, a repetition of the same forms, the same signs, which if you think about

de-, dis-, ex-.

it, corresponds to a normal ten or fifteen year cycle, time enough for new forms of practice to be generated. But the return of such a climate is also delayed by other factors. The present social crisis prevents a consensus from forming in which communal values might be reasserted. The only form of renewal in contemporary America seems to enrich the rich and pauperise the poor. In such a context, the appeal of aesthetic experiences tends to recede behind new forms of spirituality, and in America we are witnessing the burgeoning of cults and various other religious congregations. Looking back on it, one wonders if the aesthetic explosion of the 60s in America has not been bridled by this later rush in contemporary spiritual experiences.

There is also another phenomenon, which could be described as the emergence of a denigration of European theories. I am currently working on a paper for a conference in America which I have entitled 'Europhilia or Europhobia?'. Possibly not in artistic milieus, but certainly in academic and political circles, there is a progressive rejection of Europe, its emergence as a union of nations, as if the construction of Europe, were to threaten a certain idea America has of itself. What is interesting here is that this phobia is coupled with a phobia of European thought. After having assimilated European currents of thought for several decades, suddenly there seems to be a fear of having become colonised by it. Thus one witnesses the rejection of the 'French stuff' *en masse*, which is criticised by some - but thank God not by all - in extremely empirical terms, without the theories having been adequately assimilated. One has heard of a certain Mr Sokal whose work I have not read, but who wages war against Lacan, Derrida, Deleuze, myself, etc. This resembles a revolt against theory in favour of a return towards pure science. French theory has been the first victim of a caricatural use by partisans of political correctness. They superimpose their own ideological preoccupations onto texts, diverting them from their initial intentions. There is now a desire to get rid of all that but the action taken consists of throwing out the baby with the bath water. It also becomes a nationalist claim, at least this is how I perceive it, an anti-European move which may turn out to be more serious than we think, in that it is a form of cultural isolationism.

The Question of Exile

AD: In the evocation of your academic trajectory, one sees the direct consequences a political climate may have on interdisciplinary dispositions, or indeed how political factors may indirectly contribute - through the initial hijacking of fundamental liberties - to the development of very individual modes of thinking. This seems to me also suggested, - almost in between the lines - in the first part of Strangers to Ourselves *(1988), where you describe the necessity - brought about by the experience of exile - to work differently. Is that to say that one needs to reinscribe in the genealogy of the modern avant-garde, the relevance of its geographic and emotional displacement in order to understand the invention of the new sets of rules, new ways of working that ensued?*

JK: This is a very important question, full of political implications. Some people are concerned and a bit shocked by this surge of well-meaning cosmopolitanism which consists in saying, if you believe yourself to be a progressive, a liberal, a free-thinker open to novelty, 'Viva Strangers!' or 'exile is the way forward'! In reaction to this form of cosmopolitanism, in France, but not only in France, you see a turn to extreme-right ideologies as we see with the case of Le Pen. But this is also felt and heard amongst a certain number of French artists, who seem to think that the excavation of one's roots, one's own language and traditions, constitutes the most fertile terrain of

de-, dis-, ex-.

inspiration. They are not completely wrong, and certainly this redis-covery opens up interesting paths. In many ways, for instance, the national traditions going back to the Middle Ages and beyond are very fruitful when in dialogue with the development of contempo-rary art practices. However, as it happens, my personal trajectory takes me in the completely opposite direction, and as far as the cul-tural context in which we are discussing these issues is concerned, given the Internet, given globalisation, it goes without saying that thinking beyond frontiers is in our interest. Clearly, we are more and more likely to become strangers, living in a different context than the one in which we were born. It is this blending of origins which interests me. However, let us be clear: national cultures and entities are having to co-habitate in this same space, however global. An uprooting could not create anything more remote than a neutral universal code. What I tried to reaffirm in *Strangers to Ourselves* is the share of suffering induced by any uprooting. This suffering takes the question of origins into account: sometimes it is the story of a betrayal, sometimes an execution, but in any case, if the feeling of being uprooted and the ensuing pain - the pain of reintegration - are not experienced, there can be no creative work of any kind. In other words, the point is not to construct some kind of Esperanto, or some kind of abstract language originating from nowhere, but on the contrary, in order to give life to new signs (whether one is deal-ing with natural language, colours or spatial forms), it is necessary to establish a bridge from one's origins to the arrival and appropria-tion of a whole new set of signs. What I am referring to here is thus the existence of an inter-semiotic in the making, as opposed to a neutral code. I think it is important to name this process because often, when you hear about cross-culturalism or seductive terms such as 'exiled art', there tends to be an assumption that an abstract code is already in place to frame the oncoming signs. I think we can say that in the current period it is the interface between cultures which is most visible, the emergence of frictions and not their obliteration through an abstract system of signs. Thus with regard to your question on the nature of the work produced in exile, the hardest aspect of all is to find a way to remain in contact with the culture of origins, and yet to appropriate this new culture, so that a cross-breeding of the two can occur.

AD: With regard to 'the unveiling of new intellectual or artistic territories' presented as the direct consequence of exile, isn't there a certain form of romanticism at work here?

JK: This romanticism is legitimate. The main question to ask is what we mean by 'new territories'. If those are to be abstract and universal 'sites', devoid of any savour and felt cultural roots - whether individual or national - then we are in the wrong. A new site is by definition something that has to be constructed with new material, and as we know it is only through the mixing of traditions and new sensibilities that this can be achieved. But what you can see appearing now is another form of romanticism which consists in nourishing exile and the free-thinking it suggests with an emotional subtext. Many recent events, be it the reaction to the death of Diana, to the death of Mother Teresa, or the extraordinary reactions to the arrival of the Pope in Paris last summer, seem to suggest (and many commentators have picked up on it) that one way to resist the uniformisation induced by our 'society of the image', is to display strong emotions. These unexpected overflows of emotion could be read as a mode of resistance to the systematic standardisation we are exposed to through the tyranny of images. It is interesting to note that this overflow of emotion corresponds to the means adopted in various and diverse situations; be it a stand of opposition against a royal court, against the revealed corruption of a country, against the 'society of the spectacle' itself, or against institutions and their inability to deal with contemporary forms of isolation, unemployment, poverty, homelessness, etc. In itself too the expression of all this emotion takes many different forms and here, behind known signs of depression, we see many new forms of illnesses. Here again, we are witnessing the same failure of general and abstract codes: not only is the form and abundance of emotion not understood by traditional grids of interpretation, but its vibrant sensitivity becomes a certain form of counter power, a violence against stereotypes.

AD: This leads me to my last question. In your practice as an analyst, you often refer to this moment of crisis, characterised above in the light of recent events. But this terminology remains also relevant in your critical reinterpretations of literature and art work. For instance, in your interview for the 1995 Tate Gallery exhibition catalogue Rites of Passage, *you see in the art works on show the manifestation of a "moment of fragmentation". This leads me to ask you about the decision to treat the art work as a symptom, pointing to an illness, signing a crisis. Isn't there a danger, by applying to the register of art, a psychoanalytical terminology, to bypass the tangible object altogether? Can we assume the 'artist as producer of the symptom'; in other words, can we operate an interpretative shift from an artwork to the potential case constituted by the artist who produced it?*

JK: This is a very important question and there are two parts to my answer. On the one hand, this phenomenon that you are signalling does occur and is possibly very harmful to art, in that the art object becomes almost the 'waste' part of the process. Stuck in its ugliness, its formless state (around which no meaning can circulate) repels the viewer precisely by resisting any forms of interpretation.

But this is exactly when the plague of theoretical inflations comes onto the scene, and where some contemporary art historians, or theoreticians, shift their reading towards the analysis of a case. Here is a little insignificant object and from it the process of analysis is displaced onto its producer. I must say that this is never without being interesting, in that obviously, as you visit contemporary art exhibitions, you do form an idea of contemporary anxieties and crises. In the best of cases, you are allowed to enter into conversation with the work, finding a consonance with your own interrogations. But, and this is my second point, such readings can be extremely reductive, and to my mind, this attitude towards art needs to be challenged. Yet how? I think that at stake is a rethinking of the gaze. The gaze needs to be educated further so that it is taught to recognise a crisis in *all* images, whether an installation or an engraving by Goya. From this notion of crisis, I would like the viewer to, first of all, regain a fascination for the visible, and secondly, for him or her to enter the visible, that is to say, for him or for her to be able to see how much each encounter with the visible is in fact a negotiation with the invisible. Unfortunately, we are too accustomed to the spectacular, to the consumption of the spectacle. We are told what to look for and where to look for it. This is the result of an evolution in Western art which has led us to remain on the surface of what there is to see. But precisely through forms of contemporary art - and this could be the face of the 'symptom' - the surface of the object is in crisis. Contemporary installation art answers this crisis, but possibly by going too far into the invisible. We need to learn anew how to negotiate both the visible and the invisible, and this has to start with paying a tribute to the visible; it is a structuring element which is essential. In other words, the production of objects is essential. The loss of skills, such as drawing or sculpture, would have very severe consequences. There are no valu-

de-, dis-, ex-.

able reasons to sacrifice representation. What contemporary practices tell us, and it is true for art and for other forms of discourse too, is that we need to read the visible, knowing that the visible is prepared by the invisible. When we look at a work of art, we enter into dialogue with its invisible part, the experience of passion, the sensorial, what we see, what we smell, what we taste; that is the reinscription of the whole of the body into the artwork.

In relation to the exhibition you referred to, my interest in the notion of a crisis reflected not so much a desire to get rid of representation, but to change representation into transubstantiation, that is a complete mobilisation of the entire body originating in the subject's experience of the gaze. I am currently working on an exhibition at the Musée du Louvre, inspired by my latest crime-novel *Possessions*. In this novel, the narrative circulates around a decapitated woman. The Louvre asked me to curate an exhibition on the theme of decapitation (*décollation*). So, consequently, we are gathering works of art, mainly graphic works, featuring severed heads, as well as heads which should have been cut but failed to be, for purely technical reasons on the behalf of the artist. In this exhibition on decapitation, I am trying to rehabilitate what we were just discussing, that is, seeing and the necessity to see representation itself, but also the necessity to see that which is not represented, for instance the violence of death, the theme of depression, the theme of castration and many others. This project has lead me to rethink the fate of the visible in the West, for instance the importance of icons, which the Byzantines thought of not only as visual art but as a form of writing too. Thus what you see in an icon is the economy of that which you do not see. You are invited to see so as to think about that which is not made visible. There is therefore a real minimalist dimension to the icon. Its essential aspect is not present in the visible part it displays.

Thus, to conclude, my real concern when I speak of a crisis in relation to contemporary art forms is to invest representation with problems it is not traditionally associated with and which might be occulted from the history of representation. Contemporary art is visually poor: it is reacting to the point of saturation. The remedy is not necessarily a return to classical form, for in fact the 'post-modern' was the first movement to quote classical motifs. I see through the reconnection of the visible with the invisible, the reinscription of the full dimension of vision, but also, a possible site for the work of theory. In many ways, theory is pursued because something is hidden behind the visible. But we need the visible side of the equation first. Thus, let us learn how to draw again!

●

Visions Capitales, curated by Julia Kristeva at the Musée du Louvre, will run from 30 April to 27 July 1998.

Julia Kristeva's new crime novel *Possessions* has just been published by Columbia University Press.

Tête de Femme, Puvis de Chavannes, 1824 – 1898. Photo: M. Bellot ©R.M.N.

Rosalind Krauss

Death of a Hermeneutic Phantom: Materialisation of the Sign in the Work of Peter Eisenman

Cultures change; and whether we read those changes as growth or diminishment depends on our perspective - political, intellectual, aesthetic. Since the late 1950s, we have been witnessing, living through, and shaping, such a change which only now that it is fully wrought, becomes distinct for us. One simple way of naming the cultural present, the one that now surrounds us, is to say that it is post-modernist. But by that term we are merely asserting that it is somehow different from the main thrust of Western culture in the first half of the twentieth century, a culture for which modernism serves as the most convenient name. To isolate and define that change is the general subject of this essay.

At least it is the explicit subject. The implicit one is the architecture of Peter Eisenman. And given the somewhat unorthodox - not to say oneiric - procedure of generating this kind of manifest and latent content, I need to preface my remarks with an explanation.

Peter Eisenman and I lived through our own experience of this cultural shift, which is to say experienced the last ten or dozen years in critical, intellectual tandem. This relationship has less to do with whether the two of us came together for direct discussion (which, intermittently, we did), than with the fact that our two careers - his as an architect and architectural theorist, mine as an art critic and theorist - ran on parallel intellectual tracks. For both of us began by locating ourselves within the modernist tradition through its central analytical model, which is formalism. As formalists - self-professed and extremely determined - we were each involved in developing a set of what we then thought were logical elaborations to the initial model.

What we did not know in these years, from the mid-through the

de-, dis-, ex-.

late-1960s, was that those elaborations were *logically* foreign to the soil of formalism, and could only really take root in a quite different domain. We had both, of course, read a description of our situation; but since we did not yet experience it as problematic, we did not internalise what we had read. In *The Structure of Scientific Revolutions*, Thomas Kuhn depicts the circumstances that precede what he calls a paradigm shift - that is the moment when one set of theories or explanations is about to be supplanted by another. During this time the working scientist experiences physical behaviour that, within the reigning paradigm, is anomalous. In order to account for these anomalies, the scientist must append sub-theories or qualifications to the major paradigm, ones that substantially begin to cut into its efficiency as explanation. It is only a new paradigm that can - under an entirely new vision of lawlike behaviour - effortlessly account for what had seemed awkward or unruly under the old one.

As a formalist, Eisenman exhibited anomalous behaviour by insisting on introducing a linguistic model into his work and criticism. At the time he did not see this as running against the grain of formalism, only as somewhat attenuating or dilating its normal categories of analysis. What is formalism, he reasons, if not a particular type of reading, and if so how can linguistics be foreign to it?

The kind of reading formalism demanded was one that converted transparency into opacity; one that both acknowledged the work of art itself and insisted that it force or promote that conversion. Transparency is used here in the sense that Sartre invokes it to speak of prose writing as something the gaze looks *through* towards a meaning. For the prose writer, words "are prolongations of his meanings, his pincers, his antennae, his eyeglasses. He manoeuvres them from within."[1] Against this, Sartre distinguishes the language of the poet as opaque: the phrase object; the work turned thing. Quoting two lines from Mallarmé,

> To flee, to flee there, I feel that birds are drunk
> But, oh my heart, hear the song of the sailors.

Sartre speaks of "this 'but' which rises like a monolith at the threshold of the sentence," by means of which the poet (or reader) "tastes for their own sake the irritating flavours of objection, of reserve, of disjunction. He carries them to the absolute. He makes them real properties of the sentence, which becomes an utter objection without being an objection *to* anything precise."[2] The word turned monolith is the word become opaque, through which the disjunction - "but" - can be experienced sensuously as though it were a smooth pebble held in the hands, or the shiny skin of an apple.

But it is not merely towards the properties of the word/thing that the poem drives us. For even as the word is isolated as object, it is transformed into a special type of thing: a cognitive object, one that forces us to reflect upon how it is we know something. As Sartre adds, "the ensemble of the words chosen functions as an *image* of the interrogative or restrictive nuance." Positioned usually as the shear between two lines of verse, the word "but" reinforces its meaning spatially by becoming an image of disjunction.

For the formalist, a distinction between transparency and opacity was crucial to the differentiation between everything that was not art and everything that was. In this sense the formalist would oppose Sartre's inclusion of prose writing (the novel, the short story) in the category of transparency and claim that insofar as it was literature, prose writing had to have recourse to devices that dam up the reader's effortless flow towards the fiction's subject. In an often quoted passage the Russian formalist Viktor Shklovsky refers to a page from Tolstoy's journals to argue for the ethical necessity of this damming up, this thickening of experience: "I was cleaning a room," Tolstoy wrote, "and, meandering about approached the divan and couldn't remember whether or not I had dusted it. Since these movements are habitual and unconscious, I could not remember and felt that it was impossible to remember, so that if I had dusted it and forgot - that is, had acted unconsciously - then it was the same as if I had not. If some conscious person had been watching, then the fact could be established. If however, no one was looking, or looking on unconsciously, then such lives are as if they had never been."[3] To lives that were routinised or mechanised by ordinary commerce with words and things, the work of art offered a renewal of perception. Against the threat of lives that "are as if they had never been," art could force a coming-into-consciousness through what Shklovsky termed "defamiliarisation" or "making strange." It was its capacity to do so that rendered the work of art a cognitive object, one that had the power to cause in its reader or viewer reflection upon the modes of consciousness.

Shklovsky's analysis presents a taxonomy of strategies for defamil-iarisation within the novel form itself: retardation, double plotting, episodic composition, and "baring of the device" - that is, forcing the reader's attention to the actual procedures of writing, or narrat-ing, directly exhibiting the technical substructure of the story. In writing about the visual arts, particularly painting, the critic Clement Greenberg addresses himself to this same opposition between the transparent - "realistic, illusionistic art had dissembled the medium, using art to conceal art" - and the opaque - "Modernism used art to call attention to art."[4] For Greenberg, the strategies of establishing the painting as a cognitive rather than merely a mimetic object are ones of locating the defining or limiting norms of paintings, and displaying these as constitutive aspects of the medium: "the flat surface, the shape of the support, the properties of pigment." To force the viewer to encounter the picture as *first of all* a flat object, is for the painter what Shklovsky's "baring of the device" is for the writer. In its insistence on opacity (or flatness), and perforce its denial of illusionism, the modernist painting becomes a cognitive object insofar as it is internally coherent, inwardly referential to its own laws or norms, and logically distinct from everything that is not itself painting. For it is the first law of this type of analysis that the devices to be bared - the use of art to reveal art - must be distinct for the separate arts.

It would seem the easiest thing in the world to apply the same kind of analysis or systematisation to architecture. And, indeed, during the heroic period of the Modern Style, architects did produce a startling kind of opacity. Stripping their buildings of ornament, they confronted the viewer/user with material surfaces denuded of their expected references to classical and picturesque style; they forced him to experience the material *tout court*: glass, concrete, steel,...as such. There were as well strategies of defamiliarisation, as these materials infiltrated his home or his office with new sets of references: to the factory, the grain silo, the steamship, the industrial shed.

Yet there was something about this procedure that was inconsistent with the grounds of modernism. For, while we might find it attractive and up-to-date to model a house on a ship rather than a chateau, taking satisfaction in the aptness of the set of associations wrought by such a metaphor - associations to efficiency, ease of

de-, dis-, ex-.

maintenance, order - there is no logical necessity in the production of this model. It is no more *essentially* about the nature of the dwelling than if we were to say that a house is like a cave, or a nest, or part of a hive. The likening of a house to a machine may, that is, produce a temporary opacity, but it does not necessarily produce a cognitive object. It does force reflection about the nature of architecture in the same way that Mallarmé's "but" forces reflection, at an abstract level, about a certain terrain of language.

It is the same when we turn to the naked display of materials, which at first we might liken to Shklovsky's "baring of the device." For while to experience glass as glass may yield certain sensuous satisfactions, it does not drive those sensations back onto the cognitive ground of understanding which collates and connects them. And if we are told that glass-as-such or steel-as-such are merely conduits to the direct experience of the building as *structure*, the pure perception of it as a support system, we may still feel that the exposure of the building as structure is not the same as the "baring of the device" of *structuring* as a fully cognitive procedure.

It was as a corrective to this misplaced focus of architectural modernism that the formalist critic Colin Rowe published a series of essays that stressed architecture as a form of text to be read.[5] Not surprisingly, two of Rowe's central essays concerned themselves with the issue of transparency, differentiating a false from a true kind, on formal grounds. The false kind he termed "literal transparency," by which he meant a literal use of glass (or any kind of opening) to permit one to see through to the structure. The other he called "phenomenal transparency," and with this term he wished to indicate - for architecture - the transparency turned into opacity of Mallarmé's "but."

cf. Longlands
& Bell's
Façade (Unite
d'Habitation
Berlin)

Defining that type of transparency as the coexistence of phenomena that "interpenetrate without optical destruction of each other,"
Rowe concerns himself with architectural forms as a "continuous
dialectic between fact and implication."[6] For the facts of physical
organisation can be presented with enough in-built ambiguity so
that they induce a reading of those facts in terms of several alternate constructs. Rowe demonstrates this in an analysis of the garden facade of *Les Terraces*, the house by Le Corbusier at Garches,
concluding that the "reality of deep space is constantly opposed to
the inference of shallow space; and by means of the resultant tension, reading after reading is enforced. The five layers of space
which, vertically, divide the building's volume and the four layers
which cut it horizontally will all, from time to time, claim attention;
and this gridding of space will then result in continuous fluctuations of interpretations."[7] Through these "fluctuations" the building's surface is experienced, then, not as a thing - a mute object of
stone or concrete - but as a ground of meanings, multiple, changing,
addressing itself to the process of cognitive differentiation. This is a
sense of surface that Rowe analogises to the surface of cubist painting, the picture plane seen as a "uniformly active field," which
serves both as a catalyst and as the neutraliser of the successive figures which the observer experiences."[8]

The split between literal and phenomenal transparency can be
likened, then, to the difference between what can be called an actual and a virtual object. The real or actual object - fossilised in time
and space - is one thing, while the virtual object - a function of the
viewer/reader's capacity to organise and reflect - is another. Insofar
as the architectural critic wishes to make discriminations along this
virtual/actual axis, he works in tandem with the other formalists in
their efforts to distinguish literary from ordinary language or art

de-, dis-, ex-.

objects from objects of common use. But to the extent that in order to make this distinction he must construct a hermeneutic phantom - a set of readings of interpretations that he substitutes for the real object - his activity veers away from theirs. In pointing to the instance of Mallarmé's "but" Sartre ties the reader more closely than ever to the absoluteness of that word - its actual location on the page as the carrier of opposition by virtue of its initiation of a new line, its sensuous properties as explosive and disarticulated sounds. But when Rowe essentialises the facade of a building as the sum of many alternate interpretations, he is suppressing the facade itself in favour of another edifice: the facade as a pretext of stimulus for a set of mental figurations, the creation of a transcendental object. Or, when Greenberg speaks of modernist painting as tying all perceptions back into the primary datum of the picture's flatness, he is pointing to a physical fact as the condition or norm for meaning with the convention of painting. But Rowe, in analogising the reading of buildings to the reading of paintings, transforms what is physically true of buildings - that they exist in three-dimensional space and are therefore experienced through time - and makes them instead a series of pictures, framing temporal experience as a set of static images.

That these might be the problems of applying formalism to architecture was not particularly obvious in 1963, the year when Rowe's first instalment on the subject of transparency was published. To Eisenman, who was a student and colleague of Rowe, the analysis was extraordinary liberating. It was of great importance to him that the kind of reading Rowe was advocating was fundamentally different from the kind of iconographic interpretation of architectural meaning that had been practised in earlier forms of analysis. The building was not read in reference to underlying classical systems or ideal geometries, nor to sets of fundamental building types for which the present one became a newly elaborated or invented metaphor. Rowe was suppressing these kinds of meanings - to which Eisenman applied the general term "semantic" - in favour of a more abstract and generalised idea or organisation. And insofar as that organisation could be perceived regardless of specific content (the grain silo, the classical column, the villa type), it seemed appropriate to think of it as a species of syntax.

For Eisenman, formalism meant this replacement of semantics (or content) with syntax. And two practices seemed to follow, logically, from this changeover. The first was to embrace a notion of "Cardboard Architecture;" the second was to insist on treating every part of a given building as a marker or sign.

Cardboard

"Cardboard Architecture" was an epithet first applied to the work of Le Corbusier in the late 1920s when it seemed that his buildings, with their smooth white surfaces and their flush detailing, were the cardboard models produced in architectural offices, peculiarly inflated to full scale. It had the connotations of insubstantiality and a strange insouciance with respect to issues of structure. But it was precisely for those reasons that Eisenman appropriated that kind of architectural *facture*. He wanted to unload the physical envelope of all function (this column "means" support) and all semantic associations (brick "means" warmth, stability, etc.). In place of these he welcomed the associations of the "model": that is as a way of generating form, of exploring ideas, quite apart from the necessities of real structure or the properties of real material. "Cardboard Architecture," he once wrote, "is a term which questions the nature of reality of the physical environment; 'Cardboard' is a term which attempts to shift the focus from the existing conceptions of form to

Langlois & Bell

de-, dis-, ex-.

Peter Eisenman, *House I*

a consideration of form as a signal or a notation which can provide a range of formal information; 'cardboard' is a means for an exploration into the nature of architectural form itself, in both its actual and conceptual states."[9]

The Beginnings of a Linguistic Model

In Eisenman's thinking, architecture would only really be perceived as "syntax" through a "consideration of form as a signal or a notation." As an example of this we might think of what it would be like to enter a space in which there are regularly placed columns supporting the ceiling plane, and then encounter one column that supports nothing. Since the anomalous column does not function as structure, it can only make sense to use it in terms of some other function, and what that might be would obviously depend on its

context. This example, which on an extremely simple level repre-sents the procedure that Eisenman followed in House I, House II, and House III, brings us back to the remark made earlier - namely, that from the outset Eisenman was attempting logically to connect formalism and linguistics. Obviously his choice of terms - seman-tics, syntactics - begins to broach this subject. But more crucially, his notion that a thing is perceived as a sign only from within a field of differences attaches his thinking to that of structural linguistics. "What we have learned from Saussure," writes Merleau-Ponty, "is that, taken singly, signs do not signify anything, and that each one of them does not so much express a meaning as mark a divergence of meaning between itself and other signs. Since the same can be said for all other signs, we may conclude that language is made of differences without terms; or more exactly, that the terms of lan-guage are engendered only by the differences which appear among them."[10]

To understand this we might take the case that Saussure introduces in his *Course on General Linguistics*, a case drawn from a level that seems so elementary that it had always been thought of as pre-lin-guistic. This case concerns phonology for which the letters in the alphabet of a given language seem to stand as basic units - though not yet units of meaning or signification. What Saussure endeav-ours to show is that if we take the letter *p*, in isolation, we are left with an abstraction that has no relation whatever to language. For *p* divides itself, linguistically, into implosive (*p* as in the word *up*) and explosive (*p* as in the word *put*) sounds. Thus the choice of the implosive *p* already differentiates itself from another possibility - the explosive sound; and because of this distinction, that choice is already fully laden with significance.[11]

Peter Eisenman, *House II*

If we return to the instance of the nonsupporting column, we can see its theoretical relationship to the two types of *p*. First, it is not being handled as an isolated symbol (the ionic column, say, which equals femininity, or the column set free from the wall as "sculpture"); but, rather, it locates itself from within the simple binarism of supporting/nonsupporting. Second, that binarism implies that there is already in place a field of meaning within which the perception of that choice will be intelligible. The nonsupporting column is understood as a signifier ("a signal or notation") whose significance depends, at least in part, on the knowledge of everything that it is not. In the actual practice of House I, House II, and House III, Eisenman relied on the principle of redundancy to establish this binarism, to make it fully recognisable. Nonstructure can only be apparent in contrast to structure. And so, in those buildings the viewer is confronted with two parallel systems: one that holds the building up physically and another that obviously does not. So the point of that second system - its meaning - must derive from something else. The referent of "system II" cannot be to physical structure but must be to some alternate level of organisation. (It should be mentioned here that the sophistication of design in these houses is such that identifying system I and II is not a simple matter, and that given alternative readings and perspectives, the elements that make up the one or the other keep changing places.)

But what, we might ask, is the referent of this alternate system? To which the simplest answer is that it is the house that is not there, or rather, the house that is there only cognitively. As an example, we could take House III in which the markings are the traces of a process of generating the building through a 45-degree rotation. If we imagine two boxes set one inside the other, which begin with their sides in alignment, and then imagine that the inner one is

de-, dis-, ex-.

Peter Eisenman, *House III*

made to go through a quarter turn, a procedure which rips open the closed sides of the outer box, we will have a simplified mental image of this process. Lest this seem like an absurdly arbitrary thing for someone to do, we might reflect that buildings ordinarily get designed by shifting spaces around: the room that no longer "works," located left of the entry, is moved, on paper, to the right, or its axis is changed, or its doorway is displaced. The designer does not understand these changes as arbitrary because he makes them in response to exigencies of the budget, or the program, or the site. When he is finished these changes no longer appear *as changes*, for they are now incorporated into the fixed structure of the completed object. In House III Eisenman makes the fact of these changes - that it evolved step-wise through time - a perceptual datum, and further, the "changes" themselves do not refer to the traditional rationalisations, which Eisenman sees as arbitrary in the extreme. They arise from a geometrical logic, which is itself apparent due to the fact that it is marked or signalled through what we are calling system II. Therefore, the complex of phenomena that surrounds one, in this building, is seen to be reducible to something simpler, even though that simple, originating order cannot be physically experienced.

The referent system II is, then, a conceptual house, conceptual on three counts. First, because it is a virtual object, one that is "present" in conception rather than in fact. Second, because it is the indicator of a set of laws that generated it, a process of moving from hypothesis to conclusion through a series of predetermined rules of behaviour, the deductive nature of which can itself be termed conceptual.[12] Third, because along the way it presents aspects of architecture from within a set of normative statements. For example, if we ask what, normatively, is the nature of a window, we realise that the answer is not this or that shaped opening in the surface of a wall, but, more generally, the lesion of a plane. In presenting the two-box analogue to House III, I said that rotation would cause the sides of the outer box to split or rip, and thus the superimposition of the two systems leads to the production of wall openings *as lesions* rather than as "windows" formed by the arbitrary puncturing of the wall surface.

I am stressing this word "conceptual" partly because it was used by Eisenman himself to distinguish between his own practice and more traditional notions of design.[13] But I am using it as well because it helps us to locate what I said at the beginning of this essay about the ambivalence of his initial position - half in and half out of formalism. The potential of moving away from or beyond formalism, and therefore beyond modernism itself, issues from contemplation of the linguistic model, a question to which we will soon turn. But the condition of still being inside the formalist/modernist system is signalled by the word "conceptual."

This is because in focusing on a rift between object and idea, conceptualism favours the latter over the former. In Eisenman's mind it was the conceptual or virtual house that should take precedence in the viewer's experience of his building. In that sense it was only the latter that was the *real* building. The relationship this bears to Rowe's "hermeneutic phantom" is obvious: the experience of the physical forms of the house is to be subsumed by a reading of them as alternate, ideated forms. Reality is to be excavated mentally, until one is able to unearth a kind of transcendental object lying beneath it. It is the house-as-idea that will rescue the architectural work from being no more than a house-as-object, a setting for Tolstoy's lives lived "as if they had never been."

In his theoretical text on the subject of conceptual architecture, Eisenman aligns his own position with that of a generation of artists who had been producing conceptual and minimalist sculpture. Relying on what had been the usual modes of describing this work in the art criticism of the 1960s, he speaks of the way this art calls for a replacement of physicality by a mental conception. One example of this, although it is not one Eisenman himself referred to, is the standard analysis of the significance of an untitled work by the sculptor Robert Morris, which is made up of three very large, identical, L-shaped beams, each of them separately disposed within their space of exhibition. Given the fact that one is up-ended, the second is lying on its side, and the third is poised on its two ends, this analysis proposes that the meaning of the work addresses the way the viewer can mentally correlate the three forms, seeing each as a physical instance of a single master idea. Thus the L-beams suggest "a child's manipulation of forms, as though they were huge building blocks. The urge to alter, to see many possibilities inherent in a single shape is typical of a child's syncretistic vision, whereby the learning of one specific form can be transferred to any variation of that form."[14]

Actually, the meaning of this work by Morris is quite different from the one suggested above. Morris is surely calling on us to see that in our experience those forms are *not the same*. For their placement visually alters each of the forms, thickening the lower element of the up-ended unit, or bowing the sides of the one posed on its end. Thus no matter how clearly we might *understand* that the three Ls are identical (in structure and dimension), it is impossible to see them as the same. Therefore, Morris seems to be saying, the "fact" of the objects' similarity belongs to a logic that exists *prior* to experience; because at the moment of experience, or *in* experience, the Ls defeat this logic and are "different." Their "sameness" belongs only to an ideal structure - an inner being that we cannot see. Their difference belongs to their exterior - to the point at which they surface into the public world of our experience. The "difference" is their sculptural meaning; and this meaning is dependent upon the connection of these shapes to the space of experience.

It is because of this fact that one would want to place this work of Morris's within a post-modernist tradition. Because what this sculpture is rejecting is the notion of the perceiver as the privileged subject who confers significance on reality by recourse to a set of ideal

de-, dis-, ex-.

meanings of which he is himself the generator. It refuses, that is, to allow the work to appear as the manifestation of a transcendental object in some kind of reciprocal relationship to its viewer/reader, understood as a transcendental ego or subject.

The further point to be made brings us back to the phonological instance of the stressed and the unstressed p. Saussure had rejected the unqualified p as an abstraction that suggested that the applied ps (as in up or $p$ut) were merely inflections of some kind of prior ideal or norm. What he was insisting was that language is not to be found in that notion of priority, but only in the application by which the meaning of a choice arises from its difference from the not-chosen. With the L-beams, the variety of positions are like ps as they exist in the spoken chain. They are thus a set of differences that call on us to acknowledge them as we encounter them, but not to reduce them to a prior, ideated figure: the L floating gravity-free in the mind. With this art, the cognitive project is therefore redirected. It is not about the intuition of the object as a goad to or confirmation of the viewer's capacities to initiate meanings. Rather, it confronts him with a multiple set of meanings that are already in place at the time at which he encounters them.

Post-Formalist Structures
With Eisenman's House VI one finds similar redirection of the cognitive project away from the production of ideated figures or conceptual unities. Intuitively we are made to feel this from an exterior view of the house, where the formal strategy of layering, as in Rowe's analysis of *Les Terraces*, is perversely applied. Both front and back facades are constructed of lateral planes that step back in space to the "relief-ground" of a master plane - a large fin wall that expresses itself as the organising vertical centre of the structure. Yet

the felt lack of symmetry on either facade, or between the two facades, undoes the cognitive task of such a central ground or spine. That is, the master plane seems to speak of or mark a centre without performing the cognitive ordering that this form would normally provide.

When we enter the house it is once more to experience the centre as marker, again with enormous sensuous immediacy; the middle of the house is riven by a double staircase, one that creates a visual axis diagonally across the interspace. This staircase is made of two solid volumes, for both are free-standing, their sides filled in from the horizontal planes from which they spring up to the profile of their steps and risers. They are extremely noticeable not only because they are the only volumes in an otherwise totally planar structure, but also because, within a house wholly neutrally coloured, they are red and green. They are also noticeable because although the green one rises normally from the ground to the second floor, the red one "goes" nowhere. It is an upside-down stair, dropping perversely from the ceiling of a double-height space to the point that would be the level of the second story if there were access to a second story there.

The nonfunctionalism of the second stair secures the identity of both as sign or notation of some kind. The fact of this signalling is underscored by the use of colour. We understand that we are in the presence of a notation, but it is one that marks a system which resists the kind of decoding that House III had called for and satisfied. Strong centrality implies some kind of symmetrical unfolding about that centre. Throughout the model of House VI we would expect a conceptual structure to exfoliate around this axis. It does not; or at least it does not for the ordinary viewer. For House VI was

de-, dis-, ex-.

designed by recourse to topological analysis. And it is topologically symmetrical about a diagonal axis that runs through its centre. This system which is coded in the forms of the house, would be perfectly intelligible to a topological geometer. That it is not to us does not thereby drive it back into the realm of the hermeneutic phantom. For the hermeneutic phantom is intelligible (for us). It is simply not physical. House VI is physical. Its difficulty arises from its being the partial articulation of a language which is unfamiliar, although that language describes the functions of the real world and was wholly in place before either Eisenman or we encountered it. The analysis of this house cannot proceed then by means of a reduction of the complex to the simple. It is more like the translation of one complex language into another, or rather the intuition - by means of a relatively simple system of markings - of a larger, more complex totality, one that exceeds our intuitive grasp.

In House VI, the operation of coding or marking has therefore changed from what it had been in Eisenman's earlier houses. We are not involved with a set of physical notations (the virtual, non-physical structure) as their "meaning." This is because the architectural elements in House VI articulate a system rather than an object; the referent is to the dispersed field of a mathematical language in place of the unity of a single mental construct.

In that sense House VI is the first of Eisenman's buildings to break completely with an idea of meaning that is essentially formalist. When Sartre speaks of the monolith of Mallarmé's "but" he is pointing to the isolation of that word at the beginning of the poetic line, an isolation that permits one to taste for itself "the irritating flavour of disjunction." "Disjunction" is the abstract unity to which the word "but," made formally opaque, gives rise. Formalist opacity

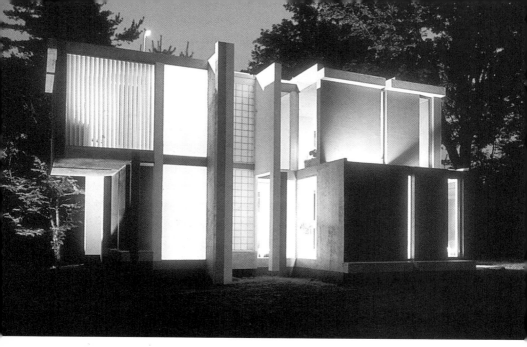

Peter Eisenman, *House VI*

depends on the isolation of the signifier (the work, the pictorial element, the architectural member) in order that it become a cognitive
object. But the abstract meaning which it then yields, takes on the
quality of an isolated mental entity. From what has been said up to
now about the Saussurian analysis of language and the insistence
that meaning takes place only through an opposition of terms
rather than the perception of those terms as absolutes, it is clear
that formalist assumptions are difficult to maintain in relation to a
linguistic model. It is structuralism which, by embracing that
model, posits an entirely different ground for meaning, insisting on
the notion of a limitless field of oppositions or differences. In this
view, if there can be anything like "the irritating flavour of disjunction," it is because Mallarmé's "but" emerges from a system that
also contains "and" and "therefore"; and its meaning is therefore
understood in opposition to those other two. If we have been char-

de-, dis-, ex-.

acterising formalism as a strategic conversion of transparency into opacity, we must understand the structuralist procedure as one that performs a very different conversion: the dispersal of unities into a field of differences.

House X is totally involved with this process of dispersal. There, for example, one encounters it in rooms with transparent (glass) floors and ceilings, and opaque (windowless) walls. The plane on which openings normally occur is thus transposed to the planes that are expected to be visually solid. And the effect of this transposition is two-fold. The first is that a certain kind of somatic shock is delivered to the viewer. He is made to experience, through his own body, the fundamental opposition in an architectural language between closed and open fields. The second effect is the view of other parts of the same building produced by the transparent planes themselves, in which other sets of opposition are manifested. The space in which the viewer finds himself is, then, one whose perspectives run vertically and diagonally through the system of the house rather than horizontally in relation to the viewer's normal plane of vision. Through this changed perspective, the occupant is forced to experience the space as a linked set of opposing terms - to encounter "the room" less as an entity than as one part of a system of differences.

To consider a phenomenon as seemingly perverse as this room, it is useful to acknowledge this space as a peculiar conversion, or rotation, of the 1914 Domino diagram through which Le Corbusier had articulated the premises of architectural modernism. The Domino diagram pictures a one-room structure, defining it with two horizontal slabs (floor and ceiling), supported by a columnar system pulled in from the room's perimeter. The diagram makes clear that any vertical plane that might be added to this space - wall partition, window panel - is utterly independent from this structural skeleton. Implicit in this diagram are some of the standard features of modern architecture as we have known it: the free plan, the curtain wall. What is also implicit is that inside this space, the occupant inhabits the conceptual centre of a three-dimensional lattice. As he stands inside and looks about, he is therefore given the structure as pure diagram, as the bodying forth of a system that is transparent to his ability to think it. The rational premises of this space are decipherable. The aesthetic pleasure it affords is tied to the pleasure of decipherment.

No matter what we understand the work of art to be, clearly one of its functions is to create an image of its perceiver - the one who looks at it or reads it. If we speak of, say, Renaissance art, we are not just referring to objects that look different from the ones that preceded (or followed) them by virtue of a set of organising rules. We are speaking as well of a different conception of the viewer and where he stands (spiritually, intellectually, politically, perceptually) *vis-à-vis* the object. The work of art pictures more than just its own contents; it also pictures its beholder. In addressing the subject of modernism, I used the example of Tolstoy's journal entry to describe this concern for the condition of the viewer, to raise the issue of the artist's sense that that condition must be attended to or revised. The man for whom everything is transparent, who is not forced to reflect upon his experience, who is not brought up short by it as if blocked for a moment by a wall, is according to this parable of the dusted/undusted sofa, not someone who has seen more of his life, but one who experiences less. Now, if a shade is pulled down over a window, preventing one from automatically using the opening to look through, one might be forced - depending on the

Peter Eisenman, *House X, Scheme H*

nature of the shade - to ask fundamental questions about the structure, purpose, and *meaning* of windows. The modernist shade was intended as a stimulus for such questions, and as the viewer responded to this stimulus he became the originator of a set of replies, definitions and interpretations. Shklovsky's formalism was put into place in the service of creating, or elaborating, the terms of this situation. Formalism was the theoretical working-out of this modernist demand that consciousness become reflexive, examining the grounds of its own access to knowledge. But, as I have said, the results of this reflection were to define consciousness as a generator or producer of meaning. Formalism's pulled down shade may have made the real window opaque for its viewer, but the aesthetically conditioned obstacle set up a new transparency in which ideas (interpretations) appear to be transparent to the mind that thinks them. Structuralism is an attack on this second-order transparency, on the idealism inherent in this cognitive "shade."

It is in the light of this attack that we can understand the rooms in House X that turn the Domino diagram on its ear, making the solid horizontal into clear surfaces and the vertical into opaque slabs. For it is the viewer's relationship to the house as a model of his own capacity to conceptualise which is also stood on its ear. The diagram is no longer oriented to the viewer as the centre of a perspective system, a system measured out on the horizontal ground on which he stands, stretching away towards his horizon. That horizon is blocked by the windowless walls, and that ground, by being transparent, is no longer predicated on the orientation of his body. The viewer may stand in the middle of the rooms of House X, but he is no longer their centre. This shade, which is pulled down over his view, is not one that returns it to him in the Domino guise of a set of theorems - about pure forms, organisational transparency, or Cartesian lattices.

This is a different kind of shade. It functions in terms of an absolute binarism. It marks surfaces as "transparent" or "nontransparent"; and it does so without returning the originating source of the meaning of this distinction to the perceiving subject. If there is anything to be read in this room, it is not a set of small-scale clues that will assist one to project for oneself the image of the house in its entirety as the theoretical extension of a root idea. Instead, it is simply the code "opaque/transparent," which one knows to be part of a

de-, dis-, ex-.

larger code, that is itself boundless. Through the glass of the floor and ceiling one can see other parts of House X. But this seeing is not the same as the "view" one had in perspective taken as a system of knowledge and prediction. This seeing is more a process of acknowledging the simple extension of the code: that it exists beyond this room and that one will in the course of one's own movements come into contact with further aspects of it.

This discussion began with the claim that insofar as Eisenman's work has been predicated on a linguistic model it has had to move further and further away from the formalist conditions expressed by modernism. The fragmentation and dispersal that occurs in House X relates to that linguistic model in a way that incorporates the notion of difference at a very deep level. When Saussure maintains that "in language there are only differences," he adds:

> Even more important: a difference generally implies positive terms between which the difference is set up; but in language there are only differences *without* positive terms. Whether we take the signified or the signifier, language has neither ideas nor sounds that existed before the linguistic system, but only conceptual and phonic differences that have issued from the system. The idea or phonic substance that a sign contains is of less importance than the other signs that surround it. Proof of this is that the value of a term may be modified without either its meaning or its sounds being affected, solely because a neighbouring term has been modified.[15]

It is this sense of language as a system without positive terms -

moreover, a system fully formed prior to any one speaker's participation in it - that has made language a model for the post-modernist (or structuralist) redefinition of man as a knowing-subject.
"In achieving a position of mastery over man," Edward Said writes,
"language has reduced him to a discursive function. The world of
activity and of human experience stands silently aside while language constitutes order and legislates discovery. When Lévi-Strauss
says that 'language, and unreflecting totalisation, is human reason
which has its reason and of which man knows nothing', he is stat-
ing the condition with which serious intellectual work must reckon.
Nearly every one of the structuralists acknowledges a tyrannical
feedback system in which man is the speaking subject whose
actions are always being converted into signs that signify him,
which signs he uses in turn to signify other signs, and so on to
infinity."[16] That this attitude displaces man from his position as
originating subject occurs "when language is no longer thought of
as a kind of secondary transparency through which shines Being."[17]

The formalist interest in the work of art as a moment through
which experience is thickened and rendered opaque must be
viewed in the light of this structuralist critique. For the formalist,
opacity is, ultimately, "a kind of secondary transparency through
which shines Being." It is a way of using the object as a lever on
reality in order to essentialise a certain part of it. It is a moment of
essentialisation or reduction back to an ontological absolute. If the
structuralists think of the work of art as opaque, this is because it is
a fragment - the partial articulation of an extended field of signs,
one of the terms in a system of differences. The energy of the work
of art is therefore seen as centrifugal, rather than reductive. It drives the perceiver's attention outward, away from itself into the vast
institution of language systems that have made it possible and to

which it refers. Eisenman's ambition is to articulate the system of differences through which architecture functions as a language. To do this he has had to take the position that architectural elements express differences *without positive terms* - whether functional, symbolic, or cognitive. His architecture has assumed the conditions of post-modernism.

○

1. Jean-Paul Sartre, *What is Literature?*, Harper & Row, 1965, p. 7.

2. Ibid., p. 11.

3. Quoted by Viktor Shklovsky in 'Art as Technique', *Russian Formalist Criticism*, Lee T Lemon and Marion J. Reis, eds., University of Nebraska Press, 1965, p. 12.

4. Clement Greenberg, 'Modernist Painting', *The New Art*, Gregory Battcock, ed., Dutton, 1966, p. 102.

5. "Text" is being used here neither in the sense of iconographic program nor in the sense in which semiologists invoke it - that is, as a nexus of cultural signs. Rowe is focusing on the abstract nature of the text, like that of a musical score, to be deciphered for its formal structure and thematic interrelationships.

6. Colin Rowe and Robert Slutzky, 'Transparency: Literal and Phenomenal', *The Mathematics of the Ideal Villa and Other Essays*, MIT Press, 1976, p. 170. Reprinted from *Perspecta* (1963).

7. Ibid., p. 170

8. Colin Rowe and Robert Slutzky, 'Transparency: Literal and Phenomenal,...Part II,' *Perspecta* 13, 1971, p. 296.

9. Peter Eisenman, 'Introduction to Cardboard Architecture', *Casabella* No. 374,1973, p. 24.

10. Maurice Merleau-Ponty, *Signs*, Northwestern University Press, 1964, p. 39.

11. Ferdinand de Saussure, *Course in General Linguistics*, McGraw-Hill, 1966, pp. 53-64.

12. Under this view the referent of the conceptual structure is the transformational process itself - that is rotation. It should be noted here the importance, often cited by Eisenman himself, of Noam Chomsky's notion of transformational grammar for Eisenman's thinking at the time. He has discussed the influence of Chomsky's division of syntax into surface and deep structure, the two levels mediated by rules of transformation.

13. See Peter Eisenman, 'Notes on Conceptual Architecture', *Casabella* No. 359, 1971, pp. 48-57.

14. Marcia Tucker, *Robert Morris*, The Whitney Museum of American Art, 1970, p. 25.

15. Saussure, *General Linguistics*, op. cit., p. 120.

16. Edward W. Said, *Beginnings, Intention and Method*, Basic Books, 1975, p. 283.

17. Ibid., p. 302.

Candida Höfer

Institutional Interiors

Bibliothèque Nationale de France, Paris 1997, Architect: Dominique Perrault
Bibliothèque Nationale de France, Paris 1997, Architect: Dominique Perrault

Deutsche Bibliothek, Leipzig 1997
Deutsche Bibliothek, Frankfürt 1997

Stadtbibliothek, Stockholm 1993
Institut für Versicherungsrecht, Köln 1989

Kunsthaus, Zürich 1994
Universität, Gent 1993

GUY DE...
LA
SOCIÉ
DU
SPECTA...

Philippe So...
L'écritu...
et l'expérie...
des limite...

Sade Dant... Lautréamo... Mala...

Théorie d'ensemble

Ro... Barthes
Le plaisir
du texte

TEL

GEORGES B...
l'expérience
intérieure

Louis Martin

Interdisciplinary Transpositions: Bernard Tschumi's Architectural Theory

With the writer of bliss (and his reader) begins the
untenable text, the impossible text. This text is outside pleasure, outside criticism, *unless it is reached
through another text of bliss:* you cannot speak 'on' such
a text, you can only speak 'in' it, in its fashion, enter
into a desperate plagiarism, hysterically affirm the
void of bliss.

Roland Barthes, *Le plaisir du texte*

The Revolutionary Potential of Architecture

Bernard Tschumi was working in Paris, for the firm Candilis, Josic,
and Woods, on the realisation of the new town Le Mirail in
Toulouse, when the May '68 student revolt occurred. At age 24,
Tschumi was profoundly affected by these events. In 1970, in collab-
oration with Fernando Montès, Tschumi published in the French
periodical *L'Architecture d'aujourd'hui* a project entitled 'Do-It-
Yourself-City'.[1] The project was based on the statement that the
success of urban life depends on the relationships established
between peoples, ideas, and objects. To improve the existing situation, the architects proposed to insert into the built environment a
series of electronic devices that would accelerate these interactions.
Communication technology could provide a new and uncontrolled
public space, new modes of interaction provoking new kinds of
human relationships. The project was entirely programmatic; form
was never an issue.

'Do-It-Yourself-City' marked a break in Tschumi's design activity;
for the next seven years he concentrated on the production of theory. In the fall of 1970 the Architectural Association Diploma School

de-, dis-, ex-.

in London hired him to teach a seminar on urban politics. Inspired both by the political involvement of the French activist architects and by the contemporary practices of the Italian radical avant-garde (Superstudio and Archizoom), Tschumi wanted to develop a theory of revolutionary architecture. In the early 1970s, in addition to regular book reviews, he wrote a series of articles on politics and urbanism, deriving his analytical methodology from contemporary French sociopolitical theories of urbanism of structuralist and Marxist tendency, particularly those of Henri Lefebvre and Guy Debord. In a first article, written with Martin Pawley, Tschumi explained the meaning of the events of May '68 for French architecture.[2] In two others, he criticised capitalist speculation for its effects on the urban environment.[3] Looking at Los Angeles and London, he showed how both cities were adversely affected by a division of the urban landscape into "sanctuaries" of homogeneous populations segregated according to socioeconomic characteristics, race, or age. Tschumi valued the heterogeneity of the city: not only did it essentially define urbanity, it also provided necessary conditions for the emergence of spontaneous uprisings catalysed by the action of small elite groups.

In 1975 Tschumi published his final article on urban politics under the title 'The Environmental Trigger'.[4] He presented the results of his research in a coherent explanation of the three ways to use environmental knowledge as a means of resistance: rhetorical action, counter-design, and subversive analysis. These had in common the intention to refuse "to come to any alliance, however temporary, with existing institutional forces." Fascinated by the revolutionary potential of the Situationist theory of actions, Tschumi was trying to keep alive the hopes of the '68 generation of architects. Nevertheless, the article revealed a disillusionment with the possibility of changing the socioeconomic structure of society. The text concluded with an unexpected reflection on architecture's autonomy, and 'The Environmental Trigger' marked the end of Tschumi's polemics in favour of urban uprisings.

At the start of the academic year 1974-75, Tschumi, who entered his second year as Unit Master at the AA, explained that "rather than analysing the variables of architectural activities," he wanted to "deliberately concentrate on the oldest constant of all, space."[5] Confronted with the failings of architecture as a revolutionary force, Tschumi now intended, with a series of manifestos, to put architecture into crisis. To understand the nature of the shift in Tschumi's research requires a brief analysis of the change in his literary sources, in particular, the move to the theory of the text developed by the authors published in the journal *Tel Quel*.[6] In the following section, the works of Roland Barthes and Jacques Derrida are taken as representative of the preoccupations of these authors - Philippe Sollers, Julia Kristeva, and Michel Foucault, among others.

Toward Poststructuralism
From Language to Text
When, in the early 1960s, Roland Barthes initiated the "structuralist activity" in various fields of production, he quickly realised that most fields, including architecture, were resistant to the binary reading of Saussurian linguistics.[7] Although Barthes wrote little on architecture itself, he tackled the problem of the meaning of the city in a lecture given in Naples in 1967. Three years later, his text, 'Sémiologie et urbanisme', was published in an issue of *L'Architecture d'aujourd'hui* dedicated to urban semiological studies.[8] Barthes considered his study as that of an amateur, and he began his exposé with a quotation from Victor Hugo to demonstrate that

de-, dis-, ex-.

someone had already intuited that the city was a kind of writing. For Barthes, the problem of semiology was that it could only talk about the language of the city as a metaphor; to achieve a true "scientific jump," urban semiology had to give to the metaphor of language a "real meaning" by emptying it of its metaphorical content. In the end, the real problem of urban semiology was that the urban signified was never definitive. As in Jacques Lacan's psychoanalysis, urban semiology was caught in an infinite chain of metaphors in which the signified is always a signifier in another group of signs, and vice versa. Barthes saw this chain of metaphors as a hidden dimension of the city - the erotic. This erotic dimension was not functional but semantic and hence social. According to Barthes, it could not be understood through sociological inquiries and polls. The multiplicity of readings stemmed from the subjectivity of each reader. For him, historically, only writers had provided access to the city's eroticism.

By the early 1970s Barthes had considerably changed his opinion on semiology. Semiology now represented the institution to which were resistant not only the different systems of signs but also literature itself. In 1973 he wrote *Le plaisir du texte*, in which he presented his theory of the text's erotic dimension. Barthes' theory of the text could in many ways be seen as a personal synthesis of the themes debated in the pages of *Tel Quel*. Establishing a metaphorical link between text and human body, he set forth the following: the text and its double - its reading - are split. This split of the object (text) is the split of the subject (writer/reader). The text being split, so is the pleasure: while the pleasure of the writer is essentially the perversity of writing without function, the pleasure of the critic is that of the voyeur clandestinely observing the pleasure of others. Barthes also demonstrated how resistance is an essential characteristic of modern literature. Looking at the economy of the work, he defined modernity as the constant attempt to defeat exchange: it resists the market (by excluding itself from mass communication), the sign (through exemption of meaning, through madness), and sexuality (through perversion, which shields bliss from the finality of reproduction).[9] Therefore, he argued, the split perversity of the modern author is to exploit the uselessness of the text and to write, simultaneously, two texts, one participating in the profound hedonism of culture and the other in the destruction of that very culture.

Unfortunately, exchange recuperates everything; even the uselessness of the text becomes useful. Barthes clearly saw the paradoxical role of avant-garde art that works against established opinion while certain it will eventually be recuperated by it. He understood that the author who wants his work to resist recuperation faces two choices: to stop writing, an act that means the destruction of the text, or to exploit the pleasure of the text. He suggested that only a subtle subversion, a "third term," could escape the structural paradigm that linked contesting and contested forms. He offered as an example the work of Georges Bataille, who did not "counter modesty with sexual freedom but...with laughter."[10] In literature this third term was pleasure, for, Barthes argued, it lay beyond ideology - "The pleasure of the text does not prefer one ideology to another. However: this impertinence does not proceed from liberalism but from perversion..." – and could not be reduced to a method or science.[11] Accordingly, the theory of the pleasure of the text could never be institutionalised because it could only produce theoreticians or practitioners, not critics, teachers, or students. In a move away from his initial embrace of the system of language, Barthes thus claimed in *Le plaisir du texte* that the transcendence of structuralism's binary system could be subverted

de-, dis-, ex-.

through textual practices.

Writing and Post–Structuralism

In 1967 Jacques Derrida argued in *De la grammatologie* that the series of binary oppositions theorised by Saussure to explain the structure of language reproduced the dominant system of Western thought.[12] Philosophy had historically developed sets of binary opposites – man/nature, good/bad, truth/falsehood, etc. – that were condensed in the dialectical problem of subject and object or, in contemporary terms, of same and other. For Derrida, this system of thought mirrored the metaphysical dialectics of presence and absence. His reading attempted to expose the theological aspect of structuralist thought at its theoretical root.

Saussure had concentrated on the spoken dimension of language, in accordance with the Western philosophical tradition that held writing to be merely a supplement to, or a double of, speech – a violence done to writing which Derrida attacked. In his *Cours de linguistique générale*, Saussure had foreseen the possibility of a new science of the sign, of which linguistics would be only one branch. In the early 1960s, Barthes had already reversed Saussure's proposition: holding that the development of semiological studies showed their dependence on linguistics, he had placed the science of language at the top of the theoretical pyramid. In *De la grammatologie* Derrida radicalised Barthes' proposition, giving priority to writing over speech in a very tight theoretical argument in which he tried to prove the historical anteriority of writing. Derrida invented the concept of *différance* to explain the evolution of writing from the reading of a hypothetical initial trace to the structure of language.

In arguing that there exists an abyss between signifier and signified,

Derrida wanted to deconstruct the logic of absolute presence. To deconstruct the whole tradition of Western philosophy meant to dislocate all binary oppositions, all dualisms and dialectics having for a unique theme the metaphysical presence. Initially, deconstruction could be defined as a reading and a production (writing) that attempted to reveal the absence of a transcendental signified.

For Derrida, once the concept of sign was dislocated and its logic destroyed, the sign reflected no definitive meaning. It was always doubling, redoubling, and dedoubling what it reflected. Writing became a game open to all manipulation. To deconstruct was to think writing as the game of language, but for Derrida this game, which was thinking the absence of the transcendental signified, was not only a game in the world: it was the game of the world. To play the game of language was to think the world. Therefore deconstructionist studies tried to demonstrate a difference between the internal reality of the "Saussurian psychic image" and external reality. The first imperative was to show the ambivalence of any reading, the plurality of meaning being considered, in the end, proof of the absence of an absolute metaphysical and pure signified. For Derrida, the meaning of the text was caught in a labyrinth of mirrors – a model similar to the Lacanian chain of metaphors with which Barthes was, at the same moment, characterising architectural meaning.

A decade later, in the second half of the 1970s, Barthes' affinity with Derrida's position appeared clearer. In the *Leçon inaugurale de la chaire de sémiologie littéraire* given at the Collège de France in 1977, Barthes reflected on his earlier activity, hence once again on language.[13] He explained how, in revealing the coded nature of language, linguistic analyses had pointed out that language was fundamentally a legislation, the place of an oppressive power that *litera-ture* alone could resist. In playing with words, in trying to express in its unidimensionality the pluridimensionality of reality, literature combatted language from within. Barthes further explained how he conceived of semiology as a deconstruction of linguistics. Linguistics in dissociating language and speech was mystified. In concentrating on the structure of language, it neglected speech and thus the rhetoric of power. For Barthes, only the text could resist power, and, when applied to the text, semiology was necessarily transformed into a nondiscipline, a nonscientific text. Barthes thus viewed the semiologist as an artist playing with signs, conscious of, yet fascinated by, the lure of the sign. This fascination was another face of the pleasure of the text, the erotic deconstruction of lan-guage.

The Pleasure of Architecture

In 1974 Tschumi tried to translate into architectural terms the con-cepts of this theory of the text, working mainly with four of its salient points: the resistance of modernity through pleasure, the research of limits, the practice of intertextuality, and the crisis of the sign. He introduced the concept of pleasure in his work with a manifesto entitled 'Fireworks' in which he stated that architecture should be built and burned just for pleasure.[14] Then, in a series of articles published between 1975 and 1977, Tschumi fabricated, in an intertextual fashion, a theory of the "pleasure of architecture." In the first of these articles, 'Questions of Space: the Pyramid and the Labyrinth (or the Architectural Paradox)', he explained that the logic of his manifesto ensued from a new definition of architectural space.[15] For him, architecture faced a paradox, an abyssal problem that was putting architecture into crisis.

The Paradox of Architecture

Tschumi's paradox and its solution were a perfected version of the Barthesian notion of architectural eroticism. He conceived it in adapting for architecture the textual theory of the *Tel Quel* group, on to which he superimposed the metaphor of "the pyramid and the labyrinth" discovered in Denis Hollier's book on Georges Bataille, *La prise de la Concorde*. Through Hollier, Tschumi came to understand the fascination of the authors of *Tel Quel* with Bataille; moreover, Hollier's book turned out to be a treasure, establishing a solid link between text and architecture.[16]

Bataille was obsessed with architecture. For this reason, Hollier analysed his work using an architectural metaphor borrowed from philosophy: the interplay between pyramid and labyrinth. More precisely, philosophy, caught in the labyrinth of experience, tries to erect a pyramid of reason (science) to overlook the labyrinth (nature) and understand it. With this metaphor, Hollier explained Bataille's offensive against the Hegelian "philosophical edifice." For Bataille, the labyrinth could never be overlooked because of the impossibility of building the pyramid, that is, reason and its invention, science, could never explain nature. The labyrinth, constituted by language, was not a simple prison, for one never knew whether one was inside or outside. Therefore, in Bataille's logic, writing was a game played with elusive reality.

Tschumi used Hollier's model to explain his architectural paradox. He argued that architecture consisted of two interdependent but mutually exclusive terms: "conceived space" and "perceived space." As the ultimate symbol of reason, the pyramid represented "conceived space," or the dematerialised mental space where matter is moulded by ideas. The pyramid was the very tradition of architec-

de-, dis-, ex-.

ture. But Tschumi held that built space affected the senses long before reason. The labyrinth represented "perceived space"; it was the prison of sensations, an elusive model of spatiality that contemporary architectural theories had forgotten. For Tschumi, following Bataille, the labyrinth's importance was that it offered no point of transcendence and was thus radically opposed to "conceived space," the space of reason. The paradox was that architecture was both pyramid and labyrinth and, as Tschumi wrote, "architecture is always the expression of a lack, a shortcoming, a non–completion. It always misses something, either reality or concept." This paradox was due to "the impossibility of both questioning the nature of space and, at the same time, experiencing a spatial praxis." To clarify his thought, Tschumi invoked a paradigm central to structural linguistics, writing that as "the concept of dog does not bark," similarly "the concept of space is not space."[17] Tschumi's paradox placed architecture within a system of oppositions that only a third term could dissolve. He suggested two readings of his paradox, one political and the other disciplinary. The political reading referred openly to the Frankfurt School and the Situationists, but also tacitly to Barthes. Reviewing current architectural avant–garde tendencies, Tschumi could explain without difficulty how the structural paradigm that linked contesting and contested forces was also valid in architecture. His solution was to exploit radically architecture's non-necessity: as a result, architecture had to be built and burned simply for pleasure. The disciplinary reading of the paradox had more tragic consequences because, for Tschumi, the sole alternative to the paradox was silence: for the first time in history architecture faced self–annihilation. He proposed that the only way to reconcile "conceived" and "perceived" spaces was to discover architecture's eroticism, in other words, to reach the point where the subjective experience of space becomes its very concept. The disciplinary implications of the paradox were a rhetorical dramatisation for the introduction of the third term of architecture: "experienced space." For Tschumi, situated at the limit of conceptual and performance art, "experienced space" was a concept similar to Bataille's notion of a deep interior experience.[18]

Tschumi's plan was clear. He read architecture through a dualist model and introduced a third term to subvert the duality. From the superimposition of Hollier's reading of Bataille on to the theory of the text found in *Tel Quel*, Tschumi fabricated his own theory of architectural eroticism. In substituting architecture for text, he was also indirectly reintroducing an up–to–date version of the old organicist analogy with the human body in which the split nature of architecture reflected both the split of the writer/reader and that of the philosophical subject (mind/body). He thus established a chain of metaphors linking architecture, text, and human body. In the end, 'Questions of Space' was a reorganisation of Tschumi's own theory of architecture. In 1970 he had proposed a tripartite reading of the city as ideas, objects, and peoples. In 1975 he argued that architecture comprised three modes of space, "conceived," "perceived," and "experienced." Bridging sensory perception and reason, architecture represented, for Tschumi, the erotic object *par excellence.*

Other Layers

In his next two articles, both written in 1976, Tschumi tried to deepen his theory by adding two more layers to his superimposition. The first was a dualist reading of the history of architecture that attempted to show how architecture was essentially a seductive representation of order. The second was a critique of modernist architecture that employed elements of Bataille's theory of eroti-

de-, dis-, ex-.

cism described in Hollier's book. With 'Le Jardin de Don Juan' Tschumi wanted to establish the historical relevance of his paradox.[19] For him, it was an invariant factor throughout the history of architecture. The paradox, which reflected the split between mind and body, was also apparent in dualities of order/disorder, chaos/regularity, rationality/sensuality, and so on. Tschumi examined the history of one architectural manifestation of these dualities: the opposition between cities and gardens. Classical or romantic, Apollonian or Dionysian, gardens were the mirror either of nature or of the city. Tschumi then associated architecture with the figure of Don Juan and presented it as a vulnerable seductress forever hiding behind the masks of different styles. Architecture, a decor built on carefully calculated laws, was a seductive illusion of an absolute order. Affecting the senses and the mind, the pleasure of architecture was so absolute for Tschumi that it could replace the pleasure of the text as a cultural model.

With 'Architecture and Transgression', Tschumi explored the consequences of Bataille's theory of eroticism for his definition of architecture as an erotic phenomenon.[20] Yet Tschumi's operation was in itself a perversion of Bataille's position. Although Bataille considered literature and eroticism as indissociable, he never associated eroticism with architecture. Architecture was, for him, the symbol of reason and a metaphor for philosophy. Hollier explained in *La prise de la Concorde* how Bataille was fundamentally acting against architecture and its central paradigm, the project, because he wanted to express its opposite, the other side of reason. His antiprojectual activity could be interpreted as the constant attempt to express the forces of destabilisation. For Bataille, this was necessary in order to understand where positive and negative thoughts intersected. He had intuited that they met where social taboos emerge. To transgress taboos was to have access to this point. Bataille considered such transgression to be essentially erotic because, for him, eroticism was the point where life meets death. For Tschumi, architecture also possessed taboos whose transgression was erotic. In fact, Bataille's eroticism did have an architectural equivalent in the ruin, which he presented as both the most erotic of objects and the symbol of the architecture's resistance to society. Obviously, however, Tschumi was not attempting a rigorous presentation of Bataille's position. What mattered to him was that the metaphorical relation established by Bataille between architecture and the philosophical text provided him with the elements to criticise rationality in architecture. He could, for example, denounce modernist architecture for its unconscious attempt to hide death. Tschumi's critical work also had specific objectives inside the internal debate of architecture. One effect of the assimilation of the structuralist thought in architecture was the emergence, in the mid–1970s, of the neorationalists, who were establishing their work on a positive evaluation of architecture's rational tradition. The exacerbation of rationality by an excess of rationality became one of Tschumi's favorite slogans.

Anti–synthesis

In 1977 Tschumi summarised his research on architectural eroticism with 'The Pleasure of Architecture' – a title that unequivocally referred to Barthes' *Le plaisir du texte*.[21] Like several French intellectuals, Tschumi was seduced by the "Barthesian" definition of literary modernity as resistant to institutionalisation. Seemingly, he perceived the consequences of Barthes' discourse on the textual and architectural resistance to semiology. He noticed, above all, that this resistance was erotic: in the text, eroticism was linked to the discovery of pleasure and the deconstruction of language; in architecture, it was linked to architecture's semantic dimension, caught in an infinite chain of metaphors.

de-, dis-, ex-.

Presented in the form of ten fragments, 'The Pleasure of Architecture' was openly an antisynthesis in which more layers were added to the theory. Tschumi introduced the notion of pleasure by paraphrasing Barthes' argument on the suspicious attitude of both the political Left and Right toward the hedonism of pleasure. As in the case of Bataille, however, Tschumi subverted Barthes' theory when he wrote that pleasure lay in "both the dialectics of the oppositions and in their disintegration." In reaching the "erotic" border between structuralism and poststructuralism, his theory was ambivalent. Moreover, Tschumi boldly associated Laugier's theory of the city with deconstructionist thought because it proposed a blend of regularity and fantasy. He also presented Kent and Brown, Lequeu and Piranesi as early deconstructionists. In addition, Tschumi used the very notion of the fragment, which he claimed to have found in Freud, to compare architecture with language. In 'Sémiologie et urbanisme' Barthes had already indicated how in his theory of the language of dreams Freud had emptied the metaphor of language of its metaphorical content. Tschumi defended the analogy between Freud's dreams – fragments of the unconscious – and architecture as a way to explain how architecture, too, is an assemblage of fragments (real/virtual). This, in turn, led him to a reading of architecture as an intertextual practice in which fragments are quotations without quotation marks.

Pleasure and eroticism were salient concepts in Barthes' theory of the text. The superimposition of this new layer on to Tschumi's earlier theory distorted the original propositions of his sources. The "pleasure of architecture" was, in essence, an accumulation of definitions establishing a network of associations; these were never built on logical correspondences, but rather were stimulated by metaphorical relationships. The logic of Tschumi's operation came from the effects it sought to produce in the realm of architecture.

Transpositions
Intertextuality

After the publication of 'Architecture and Transgression', a reader complained that Tschumi had failed to cite Thomas Kuhn's book *The Structure of Scientific Revolutions*, although he had, without any doubt, almost integrally copied a passage from it.[22] A comparison of the paragraphs revealed that Tschumi had simply replaced the word "science" from the original text with the word "architecture" in his own. He had then slightly transformed Kuhn's prose to make it fit into his article. Through this operation, Tschumi's text acquired an immediate depth. Without the quotation marks, the idea developed by Kuhn in the field of science was integrated in architecture and could be seen as an original theoretical concept. Once the appropriation was discovered, Tschumi's text remained autonomous, although it could also be read as an invocation of Kuhn's authority.[23]

A verification of his sources reveals that Tschumi made extensive use of this procedure in the construction of his texts. That he did so consciously may be seen in another example, taken this time from 'Questions of Space'. Here, Tschumi introduced his solution to the "paradox of architecture" as a proposition perhaps unbearable for scientists, philosophers, and artists alike. This description, however, employed the exact words that Philippe Sollers used to characterise the work of Bataille.[24] With full awareness, Tschumi was trying to transpose into the realm of architecture the effects sought by Bataille in literature.

Although Tschumi publicly apologised for his "oversight" after he was discovered, these articles may be read as the site of a systematic operation inspired by another prominent element of *Tel Quel*'s theory of the text: the concept of intertextuality. In his article for the *Encyclopedia Universalis*, Barthes, responding to the question 'What is a Text?' summarised the theory.[25] For him, the notion of "text" emerged after the critique of the sign, when the sign entered into crisis. He attributed to Julia Kristeva the epistemological definition of the text, which incorporated several theoretical concepts including that of the intertext. Barthes explained that all texts are made of fragments of other texts and are thus necessarily intertextual. The production of the text is a permutative operation of "deconstruction–reconstruction" of former texts. But the intertext is that which, in the text, is given, without quotation marks, as anonymous, unconscious, or automatic formulae. Barthes argued that the intertext gives to the text a productivity that is not mere reproduction, because the intertext cannot be conceived as a voluntary imitation or a visible filiation.

After his reading of Barthes, Genette, and Kristeva, Tschumi conceived his texts as collages, palimpsests, composed through the intentional juxtaposition and superimposition of fragments of other texts that were often reduced to mere *objets trouvés* whose origins and context of emergence were blurred. Together with Tschumi's technique of substituting one word with another – the title of 'Architecture and its Double' directly referenced Antonin Artaud's *Theatre and its Double* – this operation was an extreme and provocative use of the concept of intertextuality.

Tschumi and Barthes
In transposing to his field the elements of Barthes' textual theory Tschumi produced another definition of architecture. As should be

clear, this definition placed architecture within a chain of metaphors. Yet apparently Tschumi was not attempting to empty metaphors of their metaphorical content. His operation was less a "scientific jump" than a manifesto to expand and explore the metaphorical, thus nonscientific, nature of architectural theory. He exploited Barthes' definition of architectural eroticism by building a "Lacanian" chain of metaphors. Science, text, theatre, human beings, music, cinema, and architecture were connected by a network of theoretical links that negated causal relationships: one system merely triggered acts in another. This nonscientific vision of the architectural task could, nevertheless, accommodate another definition of surrealist origin. In effect, Tschumi criticised postmodernism for reducing architecture to a mere knowledge of forms while, as an art, it was a form of knowledge.[26] And, in emphasising artistic exploration in architecture, Tschumi strategically avoided the difficulty of evaluating the relevance of this metaphorical "knowledge."

The assimilation of Barthes' theory considerably clarified Tschumi's work. First, in superimposing the Barthesian pleasure of the text on to Bataille's theory of eroticism, Tschumi justified his own "Bataillean" correspondence between architecture and eroticism, a correspondence that had been indicated in other terms by Barthes in 'Sémiologie et urbanisme'. Moreover, in substituting "architecture" for "text" in Barthes' theory of textual pleasure, he could define architecture as a medium irreducible to an ideology because it was able to represent all ideologies. Inspired by Artaud and Bataille, Tschumi's discourse on sex, crime, and violence aimed to extirpate from the definition of architecture all the moral overtones traditionally associated with it.[27] Architecture's new direction was to develop an analogue to contemporary production in other fields.

de-, dis-, ex-.

Tschumi's work can also be interpreted as a research program based on the definition of modernity as "the constant attempt to defeat exchange." He first stated that architecture had to negate what society expects from it: thus ruins became the most architectural of objects. Next he began to build temporary constructions that he named the Twentieth–Century Follies, a kind of "instant ruins" without function. The Follies shared another explicit characteristic of Barthesian modernity: they resisted the sign through their lack of meaning and their direct reference to madness. Finally, Tschumi's entire discourse on eroticism mirrored a conscious resistance to ideological reproduction – the architectural analogue of sexuality.

Tschumi and Sollers

By the mid–1970s, the influence of Philippe Sollers on Tschumi's work was as direct as that of Barthes. His book *L'Ecriture et l'expérience des limites* provided a program with systematic goals and methods that Tschumi used to criticise architecture.[28] Sollers' goal was to conceive a "reading machine" redefining literature not as a work of art produced by an author but as the product of a writer attacking language itself. Sollers opposed to the traditional history of literature, which praises "good writing," a history of writing whose logic was that of a relational network similar to spatial geometry.[29] In *L'Ecriture*, he collected his earlier articles on the works of Dante, Sade, Lautréamont, Mallarmé, Artaud, and Bataille - writers that he thought had explored the limits of literature. For Sollers, their works showed the radical nonexpressivity of textual writing. These names appeared in Tschumi's work; but, more importantly, Sollers' concept of the experience of limits became a central aspect of his discourse.

After the publication of 'The Pleasure of Architecture', Tschumi reoriented his research to concentrate again on the definition of architectural space. In the early 1980s, he introduced new themes and references through the definition of spaces of desire, of performance, of limits, of exhibitions, of manifestos, of lust, of sensations and of borders.[30] For Tschumi, in exploring zones at the limits of architecture, the surrealists and futurists had initiated a work in need of pursuit. With the three–part article 'Architecture and Limits', Tschumi transposed several of Sollers' themes including the reevaluation of history and the definition of architecture as a nondiscipline.[31] One concept – the invention of new modes of writing – was seemingly the origin of *The Manhattan Transcripts* of 1977–81, a "reading machine" of architecture by which Tschumi reorganised, once more, his own tripartite division of architecture.[32] He replaced his earlier triad of conceived, perceived, and experienced spaces with a new one of space, movement, and event.

Tschumi and Derrida

The attention toward deconstruction in architecture in the late 1980s was largely the result of Tschumi's theoretical activity.[33] He was perhaps the first architect to talk about deconstruction. Of greater significance, he has convinced Derrida himself of the relevance of a deconstructive practice in architecture. Derrida's commentary on Tschumi's project at La Villette effectively validates the architect's theory.[34] Although the subject is vast, only two aspects of Derridean thought in Tschumi's theory are underlined here.

Of first interest is how Tschumi used Derrida's theory to promote architecture to the status of cultural model of the 1980s. Tschumi had quickly concluded that the pleasure of architecture was superior to that of the text. In an article of 1980, he further claimed that all that Joyce did in literature with *Finnegans Wake* Bernini had already accomplished in architecture three hundred years earlier.[35] Just as

Derrida had replaced speech with writing, in arguing that architecture was a form of writing historically anterior to textual writing, Tschumi proposed to replace writing with architecture.

A second Derridean strategy appears in Tschumi's work on the concept of *folie* (madness). As shown above, Derrida dislocated the concept of sign in demonstrating that the sign had no definitive, transcendental meaning. Tschumi attempted to illustrate this train of thought with his two series of *folies* – the Twentieth–Century Follies and the *folies* of La Villette. His initial reference was Michel Foucault's monumental work *Madness and Civilisation*, a study of the genealogy of the concept of madness.[37] Foucault's work revealed that, historically, the word *madness* changed meaning on several occasions. Derrida thoroughly explained the intent of Tschumi's endeavour. To name *folie* a piece of architecture that openly had no fixed meaning was basically to deconstruct the architectural sign. This act was, for Derrida, to decentre architecture and thus to free it from its metaphysical meaning.

The concept of deconstruction in Tschumi's discourse, like that of pleasure, has, of course, taken many different forms, and a complete comparative analysis of Derrida's texts with those of Tschumi would probably show a certain divergence of opinion. Some of these forms, like the association of Laugier with deconstruction, are not directly transposed from literature. As another example, in *The Manhattan Transcripts*, Tschumi opposed deconstruction to representation.[37] In 1985, Derrida, in his commentary on La Villette, argued that Tschumi's deconstruction of architecture was not nihilistic, because it was followed by reconstruction – a statement that tacitly relates Tschumi's practice to Barthes' definition of the intertext as a "deconstruction–reconstruction."

Conclusion

In his analysis of La Villette, Derrida provided a list of words that were composed with the prefix *trans*; he could have added *trans–position*. Tschumi often insisted, in both his manifestos and texts, that architecture was not an autonomous discipline. Yet the transposition of concepts from one field to another was a radical act only for those who believed in the strict autonomy of the architectural discipline. In effect, "transpositional" strategies marked the postwar structuralist theories of architecture and in the 1960s became typical of the discipline. Recent studies also reveal that Le Corbusier derived the basis of his purist theory from works in aesthetics, philosophy, and politics.[38] Likewise, as Werner Szambien has shown, already at the end of the eighteenth century, J.–N.–L. Durand constructed his architectural theory by paraphrasing Rousseau.[39] Thus architectural theory, in France at least, has a long tradition of "importation" from other fields. Tschumi's manifestos were not in themselves radically disturbing.

Tschumi's transpositional technique was nonetheless, strategic and more complex than this would indicate. Tschumi transposed concepts not only from one field to another, but, in establishing himself in England and America, very often from one culture to another. In a process of double defamiliarisation, Tschumi rooted these concepts out of their original context, at the same time voiding them of their inherent problems. Promoting an openly antirational position, Tschumi's transpositions were clearly not epistemologically rigorous. The goal being to create specific effects in architecture, his actions were justified by a contextual rather than scientific logic. An overview of the most obvious of these effects may yield the meaning of his transpositions.

de-, dis-, ex-.

The critical activity of Bernard Tschumi has been recognised, in the 1980s, by both political and academic institutions. In 1983, he won the international competition sponsored by the French socialist government for the Parc de la Villette in Paris. Later, in spring 1988, he was named Dean of the School of Architecture of Columbia University. In accepting this position, Tschumi was willing, at least temporarily, to come to an alliance with the institution, or perhaps he had decided to resist it from within. Whatever the case, his work is now associated with the very institution he denigrated in his early revolutionary period. His situation illustrates well the structural paradigm linking contesting and contested forces that Barthes enunciated in *Le plaisir du texte*.

As noted above, Tschumi gave a new direction to his research after the disillusionment of 'The Environmental Trigger'. His statement then on the impossibility for architecture to change the socioeconomic conditions of society was perhaps an important side-effect of his discovery of the Barthesian paradigm. But Tschumi's critical work of the mid–1970s was also a specific reaction to influential contemporary theoretical positions within architecture, among them the Marxist analysis of Manfredo Tafuri. A few months before Tschumi published his first manifesto on pleasure, Tafuri, in *Architecture and Utopia*, had analysed the crisis of the ideological function of architecture and had pronounced its death. For him, architecture was in itself a bourgeois ideology, which had been replaced, in our late capitalist society, by more advanced ideological apparatuses. Tafuri's rigorous work of demystifying architectural history led him to discard utopia as an "impotent and ineffectual" myth and an anachronistic hope for design.[40] Tschumi's definition of architecture as an artistic medium was a direct critique of the Tafurian thesis. Although sympathetic to Tafuri's political position,

Tschumi refused to accept the sombre conclusion of his theory. The theory of the pleasure of architecture, in itself a great propaganda in favour of architecture, was Tschumi's way to counter Tafuri's dead end: the seduction of architecture could dissolve traditional ideological compartments. Defined as nonideological, architecture was therefore in itself "transpositional," capable of expressing all ideologies.

Tschumi's theory of pleasure also reacted against neorationalism and Jencksian postmodernism, both movements established on the structuralist analogy with language. As we have already seen, Tschumi's reading of Hollier's thesis on Bataille provided new concepts by which to criticise both the architectural tradition and the contemporary work of the neorationalists, which gained an increasingly dominant position in the mid–1970s. Similarly, Tschumi used Sollers' proposal to transgress disciplinary limits to criticise Anglo–Saxon postmodernism. In exchanging the structuralist analogy with language for the poststructuralist analogy with the text, Tschumi did not, however, radically change the rapport established between architecture and literature since the early 1960s: more precisely, he updated it by introducing into architecture the crisis of the sign.

Tschumi's theoretical work of the 1970s was thus both contextual and deterministic: contextual, because it criticised the events of architectural actuality; deterministic, because his definition of architecture as an artistic medium implied that it should reflect on themes of this actuality. So Tschumi incorporated in his theory strictly contemporary concepts, the most fruitful of which came from literature. After he abandoned the Situationist theories, the work of the *Tel Quel* circle became his essential reference and his

de-, dis-, ex-.

key to enter the world of criticism. Following mainly Sollers (limits), Hollier (Bataille), Barthes (pleasure), Kristeva (intertext), Genette (palimpsest), and Derrida (deconstruction), Tschumi introduced into his work the major themes developed by the most visible French literary critics of the 1960s and the 1970s.

Most of Tschumi's work was shown and published in art galleries and periodicals. Through the transposition of architecture into the realm of art, which was quite popular in the second half of the 1970s, he wanted both to reintroduce architecture into the system of contemporary arts and to stimulate a metadiscourse that would decode his work. Tschumi complained that the traditional architectural critique still relied on the old category of style.[41] The concepts and themes with which he worked – the crisis of the sign, the dissolution of disciplines, the death of the author (and the birth of the reader) – were all elements integral to the literary discourse of the *nouvelle critique*. Through the translated work of Barthes and publications such as *Semiotext(e)*, the *nouvelle critique* permeated American art criticism in the mid–1970s. Tschumi meant his contaminated discourse on architecture to be recognised here.[42] His strategic alliance with art criticism became public when he brought an art critic to the design team of his project for La Villette. Conscious of the validating role of the critic, Tschumi clearly understood the mechanisms building cultural history.

In the 1980s, Tschumi was acknowledged by the authors who had inspired his work. Today he forms with them a cultural front. Any serious analysis of his position must, of course, take into account the work accomplished by the literary and cultural critics gravitating around *Tel Quel* since 1960. Such criticism could probably demonstrate the gap that exists between Tschumi's work and his sources. But this gap, seemingly a strategic displacement, could be either accepted as a necessary distortion of adaptation or dismissed for its cynicism. Tschumi, however, continues to try to produce new effects with the same literary sources. In one of his latest articles 'Architecture: Stratégie et Substitution', he laid out the elements for the discussion of a posthumanist architecture.[43] For him, the posthumanist heterogeneity of La Villette suggests new social and historical circumstances. It also marks the end of utopias, the socio-cultural and technological ones as well as that of meaning – the same three "utopias" that produced the profound disillusionment of the '68 generation. And, in fact, contemporary philosophical antihumanism, originating in the 1960s, is typical of French '68 thought. With this text, Tschumi injected into his discourse on La Villette an explicit attack on the notion of author and humanism, an attack which echoes quite loudly the projects that Sollers and Derrida initiated with Barthes in the 1960s. But, obviously, for specialists of architecture, Tschumi's denunciation of humanism has other clear meanings – such as the rejection of the old academic principles of classical architecture resurrected by postmodernism and also the Dutch architectural humanism developed by Aldo van Eyck and his followers. Moreover, as no definition of humanism could satisfy a community of specialists, one may see that here, as in his earlier work, Tschumi's transpositional operation attempts to stimulate a series of interpretations whose objective is not to develop a true and definitive understanding of his work, but rather the demonstration of its ambivalence. In other words, through interdisciplinary transpositions, Tschumi consciously inserts into the work the conditions of its resistance to interpretation. This active conscience, which is perhaps that of an author, considers architecture as a game in the world, a game thinking the world. Although this again echoes Derrida, Tschumi's work adopts a characteristic Barthesian strategy. Barthes'

de-, dis-, ex-.

ability to erect bridges between literary criticism and other fields is emulated by Tschumi precisely in order to expand intellectuals' attention toward architecture.

To a certain extent, Tschumi remains faithful to his early research. Heterogeneity and resistance are still dominant themes in his work although their early activist political edge has today given way to fragments of French antihumanist philosophy. In proclaiming the end of utopias, Tschumi seemed to adopt Tafuri's project of demystification. Like so many other aspects of his work, however, this is only a facade; for Tschumi's ascension in the academic and professional worlds of architecture may be attributed to his ability to play on the most persistent of contemporary myths. Perceived as a European intellectual by Americans and as an American architect by the French, Tschumi has profited from both the prestige of French theory in America and the legend of American pragmatism in France. Judging Tschumi by his actions rather than his rhetoric, one discovers that the eroticism of the borders is not just a playful game.

O

1. Fernando Montès and Bernard Tschumi, 'Do-It-Yourself-City', *L'Architecture d'aujour-d'hui*, no. 148, Feb-Mar 1970, pp. 98-105.
2. Martin Pawley and Bernard Tschumi, 'The Beaux-Arts since 1968', *Architectural Design*, Vol. 41 September 1971, pp. 536-66.
3. Bernard Tschumi, 'Sanctuaries', *Architectural Design*, Vol. 43, September 1973, pp. 575-90; and op. cit., 'La Stratégie de l'autruche', *L'Architecture d'aujourd'hui*, no. 176, November-December 1974, pp. 71-72.
4. Bernard Tschumi, 'The Environmental Trigger', in James Gowan, *A Continuing Experiment: Learning and Teaching at the Architectural Association*, Architectural Press, London, 1975, pp. 89-99.
5. See 'Diploma School Unit 2', in *Architectural Association Projects Review*, 1974-1975, Architectural Association, Diploma School, London, 1975.

6. Founded by Philippe Sollers in 1960, *Tel Quel* attempted to establish new methods of literary criticism.

7. Along with Roman Jakobson and Claude Lévi-Strauss, Barthes had a major influence on the application of the structuralist thought to architecture; in effect the popularity of his theory determined that the structuralist architectural researches of the 1960s and 1970s would be derived predominantly from Saussure's linguistics - a model articulated on a series of dualities (signifier/signified, paradigm/syntagm, synchrony/diachrony).

8. Roland Barthes, 'Sémiologie et urbanisme', *L'Architecture d'aujourd'hui*, no. 153, December 1970, pp. 11-13.

9. Roland Barthes, *Le plaisir du texte*, Editions du Seuil, Paris 1973, p. 40; trans. R. Miller as *The Pleasure of the Text*, Hill & Wang, New York, 1975.

10. Ibid., p. 87. Barthes was not the only one interested in Bataille. The whole circle of Parisian avant-garde intellectuals was debating the validity of Bataille's position. In the summer of 1971 Philippe Sollers brought together numerous writers, including Barthes, Denis Hollier, and Julia Kristeva, for a symposium on Bataille. See Philippe. Sollers, ed., *Bataille*, 10/18, Union générale d'éditions, Paris, 1973. On Tschumi's use of Hollier's reading of Bataille, see below.

11. Although I have given it here, I am not satisfied with Miller's translation. Barthes's sentence is more ambiguous: "Le plaisir du texte ne fait pas acception d'idéologie" (*Le plaisir du texte*, 52); see also ibid., pp. 95-96.

12. J. Derrida, *De la grammatologie*, Editions de Minuit, Paris, 1967; trans Gayatri Chakravorty Spivak as *Of Grammatology*, John Hopkins University Press, Baltimore, 1976.

13. Roland Barthes, *Leçon*, Éditions du Seuil, Paris, 1977.

14. In spring 1975 Tschumi organised an exhibition in London, inviting thirty artists and architects to make a statement on space. In the fall, the exhibition moved to the Institute for Architecture and Urban Studies in New York. See: R. Goldberg, and B. Tschumi, *A Space: A Thousand Words*, exhibition catalogue, Royal College of Art, London, 1975; see also: Bernard Tschumi, *Architectural Manifestoes*, Architectural Association, London, 1979.

15. Bernard Tschumi, 'Questions of Space: The Pyramid and the Labyrinth (or the Architectural Paradox)', *Studio International*, September-October 1975, pp. 136-42.

16. Denis Hollier, *La prise de la Concorde*, Gallimard, Paris, 1974; trans. Betsy Wing as *Against Architecture*: *The Writings of Georges Bataille*, MIT Press, Cambridge, Mass., 1990.

17. Bernard Tschumi, 'Questions of Space', op. cit., p. 137.

18. Bernard Tschumi's whole argument is formally very similar to Barthes' paradox of the avant-garde - the structural paradigm linking contested and contesting forms. The solution for Tschumi, as for Barthes, lay either in silence or in a third term. While for Barthes this third term was pleasure, for Tschumi it was a conflation of two themes related to Bataille: the notion of deep interior space and of eroticism that Tschumi assimilated with pleasure.

19. Bernard Tschumi, 'Le Jardin de Don Juan ou la ville masquée', in *L'Architecture d'aujourd'hui*, No. 187, October-November 1976, pp. 82-83.

20. Bernard Tschumi, 'Architecture and Transgression', in *Oppositions* 7, Winter 1976, pp. 55-63.

21. Bernard Tschumi, 'The Pleasure of Architecture', *Architectural Design*, Vol. 47, March 1977, pp. 214-18.

22. See 'Letters', *Oppositions* 9, Summer 1977, p. 117.

23. The correspondence established by Tschumi between science and architecture could also be seen as a pure equation of the two terms, that is architecture is science.

24. Philippe Sollers, *Bataille*, op. cit., p. 2.

25. Roland Barthes, 'Texte (Théorie du)', in the *Encyclopedia Universalis*, Vol. 15, 1979, pp.

1013-16.

26. See Bernard Tschumi, 'Architecture and Limits I', *Artforum* 19, no. 4, December 1980, p. 36.

27. See Bernard Tschumi, 'The Violence of Architecture', *Artforum* 20, no. 1 September 1981, pp. 44-47.

28. Philippe Sollers, *L'écriture et l'expérience des limites*, Éditions du Seuil, Paris, 1968; trans. Philip Barnard with David Hayman as *Writing and the Experience of Limits*, Columbia University Press, New York, 1983.

29. Michel Foucault explained the subversive action sought by Sollers in literature as an effect of his interest in surrealism. See Michel Foucault et al., *Théorie d'ensemble*, Éditions du Seuil, Paris, 1968, pp. 11-17.

30. See Bernard Tschumi, 'Architecture and its Double', *Architectural Design*, Vol. 50, nos. 11-12, 1980, p. 22; and op. cit., 'Episodes of Geometry and Lust', *Architectural Design*, Vol. 51, nos. 1-2, 1981, pp. 26-28.

31. Bernard Tschumi, 'Architecture and Limits I', op. cit.; 'Architecture and Limits II', *Artforum* 19, no. 7, March 1981, p. 45; 'Architecture and Limits III', *Artforum* 20, no. 1, September 1981, p. 40.

32. Bernard Tschumi, *The Manhattan Transcripts: Theoretical Projects*, Academy Editions/St.Martin's Press, New York, 1981; also see op. cit., 'Illustrated Index', AA Files 4, July 1983, pp. 65-74.

33. Deconstruction is always associated with the literary practice of Derrida, although it can no longer be reduced to his practice. Today, for some, the definition of deconstruction has become hazardous (see, for example, Didier Cahen, 'Introduction à l'entretien avec Jacques Derrida', *Diagraphe* 42, December 1987, pp. 11-13); however, it seems relevant to bear in mind Derrida's critique of the Saussurian sign in order to understand Tschumi's ambition for architecture.

34. Bernard Tschumi, *La Case vide: La Villette*, with essays by Jacques Derrida and Anthony Vidler, Architectural Association, London, 1985.

35. Bernard Tschumi, 'Joyce's Garden in London: A Polemic on the Written Word and the City', *Architectural Design*, Vol. 50, nos. 11-12, 1980, p. 36.

36. Michel Foucault, *Madness and Civilization: A History of Insanity in the Age of Reason*, Random House, New York, 1965. French edition published in 1961.

37. Bernard Tschumi, *Manhattan Transcripts*, op. cit., p. 8.

38. See Kenneth E. Silver, 'Purism Straightening Up after the Great War', *Artforum* 15, no. 7, March 1977, pp. 56-63.

39. Werner Szambien, Jean-Nicolas-Louis Durand, 1760-1834: *De l'Imitation à la norme*, Picard, Paris, 1984, p. 85.

40. See Manfredo Tafuri, *Architecture and Utopia: Design and Capitalist Development*, MIT Press, Cambridge, Mass. 1976. Italian edition published in 1973.

41. Bernard Tschumi, 'Architecture and Limits I', op. cit., p. 36.

42. Kate Linker provided a beautiful example of the possibilities offered by Tschumi's work in 'Bernard Tschumi: Architecture, Eroticism, and Art', *Arts Magazine* 53, no. 3, November 1978, pp. 107-9.

43. Bernard Tschumi, 'Architecture: Stratégie et substitution', *Diagraphe* 43, March 1987, pp. 107-9.

44. For a brief analysis of the work of this movement, which based its theory on a reading of Nietzsche, Heidegger, Marx, and Freud, see Luc Ferry, and Alain Renault, *La Pensée '68: Essai sur l'antihumanisme contemporain*, Gallimard, Paris, 1985; trans. M.H.S. Cattani as *French Philosophy of the Sixties: an Essay on Antihumanism*, University of Massachusetts Press, Amherst, 1990.

Timothy Martin

De-architecturisation and The Architectural Unconscious:
A Tour of Robert Smithson's Chambers and Hotels

No one can have had more perverse reasons for describing the lineaments of gratified desire.[1]

Both the American sculptor and writer Robert Smithson and the French psychoanalyst Jacques Lacan have developed a theorisation of the 'subject'. While neither was aware of the work of the other, what may make both theories comparable is their presentation of the subject as fundamentally split. The subject had at its centre an 'alien' (Smithson) or 'Other' (Lacan), which was defined as the place of the unconscious.[2] In Smithson's case, this conception of the subject as split contrasted vividly with the then current work of formalist critics of art, who emphasised artistic achievement through mastery, unity and rationality. For Lacan and Smithson, representations of the subject as unified were regarded as wishful thinking, as an imagined ideal rather than an encountered fact. In taking up the theoretical elaboration of the split in the subject Smithson was particularly occupied by the structural qualities of vision, and how this structure might be applied to an understanding of the functioning of visual desire. Smithson also recorded and documented a number of tours and trips, such as *Hotel Palenque*, in which a way of looking at a place or building was often of primary concern. What was seen (or not) on these trips was so often an unspecular 'Other' and its attendant unconscious drives. This paper will first seek to outline Smithson's conception of the subject, in order to provide a basis for understanding his 'art of looking' at buildings as a receptacle of 'unconscious drives'.

For Smithson and Lacan, the subject was obliged to apprehend itself as split in order to take possession of itself. The two components of this split were given as an 'ego' which jubilantly mis-recognises itself as a master of language, as well as an 'Other' unconscious manifesting itself through the fabrication of objects, speech, or writing.[3] For both, this Other could be found at work in art, and particularly for Smithson, in sculpture and architecture. When defining the subject as split both Smithson and Lacan were directed by structuralism, with the result that they incorporated a subjectless model of vision based on a formal system of differences. Consequently, Smithson was not just seeking to make works that stimulated a subject's or spectator's desire. He also sought to demonstrate the mechanism of desire, its structural and material functioning. Of the two theorists, it was perhaps Lacan who best summarised this knot of relations between subject and subjectless structure in his well-known dictum "Man's desire, it is the desire of the Other."[4]

I propose here to examine one of Smithson's sculptures from 1965, and then his chance encounter in 1969 with the rural Mexican architecture of *Hotel Palenque*, in order to show how they played out a conception of the subject worth comparing to Lacan's theorisation of fantasy desires and unconscious drives. The building in question so absorbed his interest that he delayed his tour around the Yucatan region of Mexico in the company of artist Nancy Holt (Smithson's spouse) and his art dealer Virginia Dwan. Their pre-arranged purpose was to visit Mayan and Aztec archaeological sites.[5] Yet, as will be discussed, this was a tour led primarily by desire, a tour which found satisfaction somewhere other than had been expected. Through his documentation of this building, and the lecture he gave to architecture students of the University of Utah about it, he took the building as an example of the functioning of the architect's 'unconscious drives.'

In order to pursue the parallels between Smithson and Lacanian theory, it is helpful to insert several of Lacan's mathemes. These mathemes were a form of notation that allowed Lacan to topologically delineate structural relations within the psyche. The mathemes used here are, in order of discussion, the barred subject [\$], the gaze [object a] and the barred Other [Ø]. In the course of the discussions below, the mathemes are marked in brackets. They provide a way of organising some of Smithson's elaborate allegorical writings and are here used as models to suggest possible theoretical mappings of Smithson's concerns.

In exploring Smithson's exposure to 'unconscious drives' in architecture, it is helpful to start by reconstructing one of his most important sculptures. *Enantiomorphic Chambers* was shown in 1966, and provided Smithson with his first general acclaim while also locating him as a founding member of Minimalism. Unfortunately, this sculpture has been lost since its first exhibition, although photographs, drawings and written descriptions of it still exist. In this sculpture Smithson's elaborates his notion of the subject who - in common with Lacan's theory of 'the gaze' - is defined as a desiring subject by his/her activity as a viewer.

Enantiomorphic Chambers

Smithson's interests in this piece of sculpture span at least a three-year period, in which he produced drawings, a draft article, an exhibition catalogue entry, as well as other items.[6] The left- and right-hand units, which comprise this work, were made of painted steel and mirrors. When seen head-on from a distance, Smithson wished the work to be camouflaged as a flat green painting with a blue frame. At odds with this flatness, two mirrors were placed forward and at right angles to the wall, one in each chamber, so that they reflected each other. Whether the mirrors were parallel or slightly oblique, or adjustable between both, remains unclear.[7] The two

de-, dis-, ex-.

Robert Smithson in front of *Enantiomorphic Chambers*, 1965.
Courtesy of the Robert Smithson Estate

units were hung on the wall so that the spectator could also approach and stand between the mirrors. Smithson remarked, "In this work, the vanishing point is split, or the centre of convergence is excluded, and the two chambers face each other at oblique angles, which in turn causes a set of three reflections in each of the two obliquely placed mirrors."[8]

Thus, of immediate note in the work, is the presence of mirrors, but mirrors set to avoid the possibility of the spectator finding the self-reflection normally expected in a front-facing mirror. Given that Smithson's texts of this time were regularly attacking the 'Humanist self' or unified ego, it would seem that the mirrors were set to thwart the appearance of the ego, depriving the spectators access to a unified gestalt self-image. Smithson does not ask the spectator to be present as a separate unity or whole, thus he effectively sidelines the narcissistic ego and its system of imaginary identifications.

Indeed, one of the many features of what Smithson often called his

"Mannerist" aesthetic was the general suspicion expressed about the existence of an ego or 'self' as defined by Western metaphysics. He followed instead the growing belief that the study of the signified (i.e. the ego's attempt to rationalise) should give way to a study of the signifier. In these suspicions, Smithson was one among many at the time. Similar claims were also being made by Arnold Hauser's book on the crisis of the Renaissance, Jacques Derrida's *Of Grammatology*, Alain Robbe-Grillet's *Nature Humanism Tragedy*, Wylie Sypher's *Loss of the Self in Modern Literature and Art*, Roland Barthes' 'Death of the Author', and finally Claude Lévi-Strauss' *The Savage Mind*.[10] Some idea of Smithson's understanding of the subject might be found in an unpublished text of 1967:

> The notion that artists have 'deep feelings' and 'pure souls' is simply a way to keep the artist in his mythic state of isolation. The first-person role that the artist is forced into by the humanist is just another way to confuse 'art' and 'life'.... Most statements by artists today are in the first-person. Until these 'I' centered statements are abolished — artists will continue to be judged according to some critic's personal notion of history. The artist should be an actor who refuses to act. His art should be empty and inert. Self-expression must be avoided. Art should eliminate value, and not add to it. 'Value' is just another word for 'Humanism'.[11]

In the light of this general distrust of certain predominant models of the subject, Smithson began to piece together an alternative. I propose that *Enantiomorphic Chambers* provided this alternate subject as a 'split' or 'barred' subject, as Lacan called it. The nature of

de-, dis-, ex-.

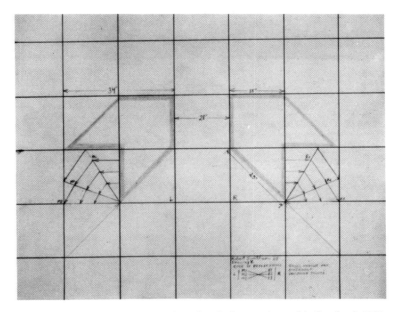

Robert Smithson, *Drawing Y* (Study for *Enantiomorphic Chambers*), 1965.
Courtesy of Jon Weber Gallery

the split which Smithson saw was given a diagrammatic form at the bottom of a drawing for the sculpture in *Drawing* Y of 1965. At the bottom of *Drawing* Y, Smithson used the pronoun 'ME', transcribing the ego into a diagrammatical 'code of reflection'. As in figure 1 below, the ego, the 'ME', has been split into two letters.

It would seem, again from the drawing, that the positions marked as 1 through 3 were different viewing angles, providing

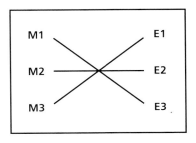

Figure 1

the spectator's nose was placed near the forward-most point of one or the other chamber. Each of these three viewing axes produced a different optical effect and each will be discussed, in turn, below. The most straightforward is the M2-E2 axis, and as it most directly critiques the disputed 'self', it will be addressed first.

M2-E2 Axis, or the Cartesian Ego

The M2-E2 axis was defined when the spectator stood or leaned between the mirrors and faced one or the other mirror with one eye closed. In their oblique setting, the mirrors then produced the first three reflections of an infinite regression. Restricting the regression to three reflections meant that the spectator could accurately remark "I see myself seeing myself," exposing him/herself - through the mirrors - to a *mise-en-abîme*. This position provides a quite literal visual situation in which the spectator is caught apprehending him or her self. This self-apprehension, at the level of thought, proved for Smithson to be the basis of a good deal of Western philosophy, particularly the Cartesian ego, but perhaps more importantly in the mid 1960s, the basis of Clement Greenberg's conception of the self-reflexive. *Enantiomorphic Chambers* was meant to turn 'self-reflexivity' into a concrete situation rather than using it as a linguistic metaphor for an artistic practice. In providing this opportunity to enter a visually self-reflexive field, the desired effect on the spectator seemed to demonstrate the failure of Greenberg's aesthetic theory of High Modernism, placed at the service of a masterful unified-ego subject. As Lacan observed, seeing oneself is not so easily done. This sculpture, when camouflaged as a painting, might be within the spectator's grasp. However, in approaching the chamber's sculptural dimensions, the subject somewhat lost its place. The spectator's gaze was not returned, but deflected to some peripheral and unseen position. Elided in this way, the subject's

de-, dis-, ex-.

place became uncertain.

Smithson started with a restriction of the M2–E2 axis ultimately to allow a third reflection, enabling this ego or 'self' to emerge: the three subjects present in the "I see myself seeing myself." It may very well be correct, though, that as witnessed by some of Smithson's friends at this time, there existed a second setting to the M2-E2 position. In this slight modification, the mirrors would have been set parallel, so that the infinite regress was as deep as possible. In that Smithson regularly wrote about Borges' paradoxes of infinite regress, and about the effects of entropy in repetition, it would seem likely that this parallel setting was of considerable further interest. I suggest that this slight adjustment of the mirror was meant to 'call the ruse' of the conscious thinking ego and its misrecognition of itself through the practice of self-reflexivity.[13] In that it created an ever-extending sequence in which a subject perceived an object that in turn perceived a subject, ad infinitum, the M2-E2 axis, in its second setting, possessed an ego-annihilating power. Smithson was not alone in using this demonstration of infinite regress to criticise idealist models of subjectivity, in which the 'self' is located ever deeper in a sequence of self-perceptions. Smithson was most likely to have encountered this same argument in his reading of A.J. Ayer and phenomenology, if not in the literature of sciencefiction.

Smithson's retort to the self-possessed gestalt ego, as he saw it advocated in Greenberg's writings in particular, was to propose the subject as split. Inside this subject there is not a true 'being' which one can grasp, but an object. By object, Smithson meant to make several points. The first sense of an inner object is the materialist one of a neurological brain entity with its accompanying perceptual physiology. One of Smithson's more memorable comments to this effect read "concepts are so much sludge collapsing down the side of my brain."[14] Smithson also proposed to locate a split in the subject between the ego and the unconscious. Smithson was of the opinion, much like Freud and Ehrenzweig, that the subject was self-divided and disputatious. This split was particularly given shape in his promulgation of the practice of "dedifferentiation" as a means of approaching the unconscious by the dissolution of all "rational categories" produced by the ego.[15]

In abandoning the M2-E2 axis, and the philosophical tradition he associated with it, Smithson was in pursuit of an alternative conception of the subject and vision. For example, he remarked in the Finch College catalogue, that "to see one's sight means visible blindness," insisting therefore on some of the qualities of the work in the light of a specifically "binocular" vision. His aim was to get around what he regarded to be a monocular metaphysical view of the subject's identity as found in the M2-E2 axis. By way of an alternative, he became absorbed in the study of the material properties of binocular sight, and the use of both eyes in the mechanisms of spatial perception. Smithson treated this sculpture, above all, as a demonstration of the physical qualities of ocular splitting, but it was also meant to lead on to show how a desiring vision could only arise once this split had taken place.

M1-E3 or the Axis of the Barred Subject [$]
The M1-E2 axis was defined when a two-eyed spectator looked into one of the chambers, again with the nose near the forward-most point of the work. In this situation, one eye registered an angled rear surface, while the other registered the inner corner of the chamber as reflected in a mirror. The various angles and shapes of

de-, dis-, ex-.

the chamber ensured that the two images which resulted were quite similar; the blue frame around the work would then appear to be in the same place in both images, while the green surfaces would appear at the same distance but at different angles. When standing very close to the work this overlapping of the two different images was absolute. The phenomenon of such doubling in the vision of the spectator provoked an unexpected 'either/or' choice between the conflicting images. The two images could be experienced only fleetingly as a unity due to a fundamental and natural structural split. After some effort, however, the two images could be made to coalesce enough for the viewer to see a unified but non-existent space, a prism-shaped area which certainly could be perceived quite without metaphor, but could not be entered, because just like the ego, it belonged to the realm of an optical illusion.

It was this persistent split that Smithson wished to identify in order to locate the subject, and which he urged the spectator to see. He found that a subject's perception of the world required the work of two eyes, two divergent points. There are, then, for this split subject, or [$], two perceiving eyes, and this mirroring in the structure of perception says something about the material composition and necessity of a gap in the human subject. Smithson pointed out that mirror splitting existed at all levels of natural structure, be it mineral, vegetal or animal. This included, as well, the dialectical structure of abstract thought and language. In the case of the *Enantiomorphic Chambers,* this split subject was produced all the more clearly by separating each eye's vision so that it saw two slightly divergent images.[16] With this sculpture, the spectator was invited to experience a certain lack of unity while remaining cognisant of the strong ego-based urge to unify the split. Having found a way to optically unify the divergent images, the spectator was made to encounter unified space as a 'fake'. Like the ego, this unified space was an illusion made possible by an anterior split.

Up to this point, Smithson's articulation of the subject as split emphasised the biological and material quality of the latter. This split, according to Smithson, was already in place and at work in society, in language, in vision, and in matter itself.

Part of Smithson's elaboration of the split in the subject extended to matters of social philosophy. He observed the way in which economic and political institutions negated or alienated the subject at the level of the commodity or sign. Splitting also arose when the subject realised that no socially recognised signifier was sufficient to represent or name the subject. Language completed the alienation of the subject, thus leaving behind a subject in search of the object of poetry, or a heap of material language. "Look at any word long enough and you will see it open up into a series of faults.... This discomforting language of fragmentation offers no easy gestalt solution; the certainties of didactic discourse are hurled into the erosion of the poetic principle.... Poetry is always a dying language but never a dead language."[17]

Smithson had quite a bit to say about this split or gap, often arguing his point against Clement Greenberg or Michael Fried. This gap was, at the time for Smithson, a major feature of the subject, and was present no less in matter.

> The fact remains that the mind and things of certain artists are not 'unities', but things in a state of arrested disruption. One might object to 'hollow' volumes in favour of 'solid materials' but no materials are

solid, they all contain caverns and fissures.... By refusing 'technological miracles' the artist begins to know the corroded moments, the carboniferous states of thought, the shrinkage of mental mud, in the strata of aesthetic consciousness. The refuse between mind and matter is a mine of information.[18]

The point in mining this gap in the subject seemed to have been that, located in this interval, were to be found the very causes of desire. Smithson saw it as advisable to enter this gap or void because desire arose out of it. Lacan proposed that, in order to initiate desire in the split subject, it was necessary for a third term to arise which he called the cause of desire or [object a].[19] In language, Smithson likened this cause of desire to the material object of poetry. As will be discussed, in vision it was likened to a vanishing point, a mirror space, and most importantly in the case of this sculpture, to a gaze.

From the split, Smithson wanted to draw attention to the mechanism through which the subject could enter the realm of desire: in splitting, the subject gives rise to the structure on which desire can be read. The object becomes here another word for the object of affection potentially capable of triggering off the subject's desire. When a thing is seen through the consciousness of temporality, it is changed into something that is nothing. This all-engulfing sense provides the mental ground for the object, so that it ceases to be a mere object and becomes art. The object gets to be less and less but exists as something clearer. Every object, if it is art, is charged with the rush of time even though it is static, but all this depends on the viewer.

M3-E1 or the Axis of the Split Subject [$] and the Gaze [object a]

What Smithson proposed in this sculpture was a gaze that lay more in the domain of desire and captivation. What this desiring gaze sought, as a way of satisfying the subject, was the fantasy of another pair of eyes gazing back. There was an experience from this sculpture of, as he put it, "being imprisoned by the actual structure of two alien eyes."[21]

Smithson's conceptual treatment of art as something that possessed a gaze was quite substantially different from conceptions found in formalist and expressionist criticism. Indeed, he may have benefited at this time from his association with the painter Ad Reinhardt.[22] Of particular relevance is Reinhardt's drawing, *How to Look at Modern Art in America* of 1946 which presented a cartoon posted on to the 'tree' of American art. In this cartoon, a seemingly self-possessed spectator points to an abstract painting and remarks: "Ha Ha, what does that represent?" Much to his surprise, however, the spectator is jolted by the painting, which comes to life, glares back and retorts, "What do you represent?" Like Reinhardt's cartoon painting, and Lacan's analysis of the anamorphic skull in Hans Holbein's *The Ambassadors*, Smithson's *Enantiomorphic Chambers* possessed a gaze, which we may investigate by following the M3–E1 axis.[23]

The M3-E1 axis, on which this gaze appeared, took place when a two-eyed spectator, with nose still close to the forward-most point, looked in a direction parallel to the wall. On this axis, one eye registered the wall as it receded away from it. The other eye registered the green interior of the chambers as infinitely reflected in the mirrors. This overlapping of images, or doubling of vision, produced a vanishing point of infinite reflections on top of a recession in the real space of the room in which the sculpture was hung. Regarding the effect of this axis, Smithson recalled a sense of capture by "two alien eyes," and of there being something which gazed back at the spectator as a result of the desire inherent in the act of looking. Looking down this axis was the spectator's own tantalising chance to see the gazing eyes of this "alien." But there seems to have been one problem in seeing these eyes: both of the conflated images were the product of a permanent recession and could not, as such, be seen. One looks and looks for this gaze, struggles with each eye to get the vanishing points to coincide, only to conclude that it is so irreconcilably split as to be unspecularisable, or simply not there. Smithson's explanation that the spectator was "transported behind the picture plane" to encounter or become the gaze seems not to be true.

The time had come for the spectator to walk away from the work, even if this required an admission of failure in respect of seeing this gaze. Thus it was in the passing of time, in the walking away and turning around, in the time it took to re-acquire 'normal' spatial perception, that the gaze became visible. The spectator was made to see the *Enantiomorphic Chambers* hanging on the wall like *a pair of glinting green eyes gazing back.*

If this final axis was the intended way to look at this sculpture, it remains to be fully said why Smithson saw this axis as the one on which desire appeared. In answering this, it should first be indicated that the effect of the function of desire here was distinctly the effect of a retroaction. Smithson, as it were, bid the spectator to wait and walk before this gaze could be seen. Likewise, he waited a moment before producing his *Afterthought Enantiomorphic Chambers* (1965) in order to make explicit the eroticism implied by the M3-E1 axis. In the centre of this photo-collage and drawing, Smithson placed a photograph of an unspecified male figure, with his head down and back turned, seemingly engaged in auto-erotic stimulation, directly referred to in the drawing as "Pocket-polo." Either side of this faceless, 'blind', and presumably libidinous figure, Smithson placed a photograph of a chamber. While the spatial location of figure and sculpture is ambiguous, ink lines connect the two chambers to form a visual intersection over the torso. Somewhere in this intersection, someone was present to a gaze. But who is this figure? Is it some imaginary spectator, or is it possibly the artist disguised as this seemingly 'alien' Other? Given that the figure wears the same clothes as Smithson does in the photograph of the *Enantiomorphic Chambers* (1965), there is a strong likelihood that the headless figure is also the artist himself.

For Smithson, sighting the Other was best done outside the gallery, away from his own work and alienation. It was an activity best practised when outside the confines of the urban landscape, when out 'on tour'. To engage with the 'alienated subject' Smithson favoured leaving New York. In a more peripheral site, it was easier to establish a more distinctly structural understanding of such relations.

The Hotel Palenque and "De-architecturisation"
The slide lecture for the architecture students of the University of Utah caused something of a stir in its original setting in 1972. Perhaps it "began a little as a schoolboy joke" whereby Smithson returned from the Yucatan not with pictures of ruins of a lost America, but with photographs of a seedy hotel.[24] Certainly, it was not an anticipated analysis, constantly buoyed by the apparent and unexpected quality of pleasure Smithson took in documenting the hotel. In his manner of addressing the students Smithson sought to

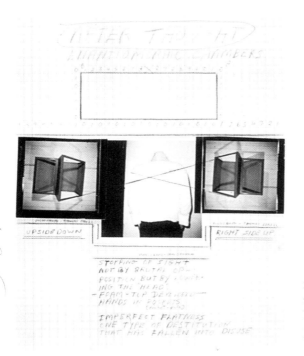

Robert Smithson, *Afterthought Enantiomorphic Chambers*, 1965. Courtesy of Jon Weber Gallery

provoke from them a realisation of their own sense of being split, as subjects having already encountered the limits of Modernist architectural logic. Like *Enantiomorphic Chambers*, *Hotel Palenque* was a lure into the possibility of seeing the gaze. It emphasised the impossible nature of an encounter with the Other as unconscious. In the lecture, Smithson set up a dynamic between his desire to present the Hotel Palenque to the students and his desire to surface the Mexican architect's and builders' decision to abandon the working site in its unfinished state. Smithson identifies the law of entropy at work, which conceals the architect's desire to leave the hotel in an ominous unfinished state, in such a way that we may be able to

Robert Smithson,
from *Hotel Palenque* series,
1969.
Courtesy of Jon Weber
Gallery

detect the very death drive of the architect. It is almost as if behind the state of entropy lurks an 'architectural unconsious'. The visit to the site caused some anxiety as to one's status as a welcomed guest:

> There is something about Mexico, an overall hidden concealed violence about the landscape itself. Many artists and writers have gone to Mexico and been completely destroyed.... So you have to be careful...that you are not caught up in...any of this subconscious, dangerous violence that is really lurking in every patch of earth.[25]

While on the road, the Other showed a devouring gaze. Once parked, it was as if this devouring had become much closer to hand and less metaphoric. If there was a note of anxiety about the Hotel Palenque, it was made all the more palpable through the genealogy

Smithson traced for it: the Mayan and Aztec architects who had provided the stage for ceremonies of mass human sacrifice were still building, re-enacting archaic unconscious drives.

Smithson found this hotel in Mexico in 1969 while on a trip that also resulted in his text piece *Mirror Travels in the Yucatan*. He described the process of finding this hotel and the sites of his "mirror displacements" as one in which one underwent a splitting in response to the materials of the site.

> When I get to a site that strikes a kind of timeless chord, I use it. The site selection is by chance. There is no wilful choice. A site at zero degree, where the material strikes the mind, where absences become apparent, appeals to me, where the disintegration of space and time seems very apparent. Sort of an end to self-hood...the ego vanishes for a while.[26]

Arriving at the hotel, however, seemed to signal an important shift. No longer in pursuit of a gaze, Smithson took up the position of a cognisant subject. This position was to constitute an artwork in its own right:

> A great artist can make art by simply casting a glance. A set of glances could be as solid as any thing or place, but the society continues to cheat the artist out of his 'art of looking', by only valuing 'art objects'.[27]

Indeed, he seems to have spent a good portion of his stay lounging in the restaurant beside the dysfunctional pool, compiling an extensive record of photographs and drawings of the buildings. Visiting the Hotel Palenque was about articulating an art of looking, about casting a glance in pursuit of the Other. Smithson often lingered unexpectedly on odd patches and dark corridors. The Architect, as 'Other', seemed to be nowhere present, yet everywhere at work: "[The Hotel] just grew up sort of like a tropical growth, a sort of Mexican geologic man-made wonder." While nobody was seen to toil, there was still some expectation that "something was about to take place. We were just kind of grabbed by it. You just really felt that any minute something was going to happen."

In response to the anxiety of being "completely destroyed" by Mexico, elaborating a theory of the gaze might seem of little help. Yet this is what Smithson called upon. One way of not letting the subject be overwhelmed by this sense of an 'Other' was for Smithson to take the position of the guide. He placed himself in this position, meticulously keeping his eye on the materials and processes used in making the Hotel. From this position he delighted in the complete lack of logic in the building. There was no centre, no plan: "The logic of the whole place is just impossible to fathom." In addition, entropy was everywhere. As he put it, "You can see that instead of just tearing it all down at once, they tear it down partially so you're not deprived of the complete wreckage situation." In view of the lack of logic, plan or completion, Smithson's somewhat unexpected response was to marvel at the Hotel. By embodying a potential guest able to admire and enjoy the hotel as it stood, Smithson effectively engaged with the 'architectural unconscious' of the hotel. Many parts of the building set off a state of excitation: a pool, a dance hall, an odd window, or a back door, all seemed to be present by virtue of an "incredible necessity."

An example of Smithson's analysis of the 'architectural unconscious' of the Hotel Palenque may be found in his consideration of its swimming pool. He found that the swimming pool had been constructed in order to bid the guest to take a swim, yet no-one wanted to swim. It had all been a case of mistaken desires. But this miscomprehension was of no importance, because the final structure was, in any case, cracked and made of rocks sharp enough to cut. The pleasures of swimming were better left as fantasies. The pool had been built so that it blocked access to another area, thus necessitating an odd rope bridge over the pool in the style used for Mayan ceremonial burial pits. What had originally been designed to be at the service of the pleasure of swimming ended up connoting deathly intentions. Smithson pointed out that the 'architectural unconscious' of the site was in fact constitutive of an accumulated architectural memory that kept cropping up accidentally, like a slip of the tongue. It was as if the architect had meant to say 'Modern pool' but had said 'Mayan pit' instead.

Returning to the lecture, Smithson offered further observations on the unconscious Other and its drives. He recounted several "meditations" on parts of the building, taking in what he called the areas of "de-architecturisation." These areas showed a breakdown of the logic of architecture leaving more evident the architect's fulfilment in arresting the process of architecturisation. This gratification seemed to be based on a surprisingly loose definition of architectural objects.

> At one point they evidently decided to build some floors, and decided that that wasn't a very good idea so they demolished them, but left this spiky, irregular cantilevered effect coming off the side of the wall.... I rather like this technique. It is a "de-architecturisation"

you might say…. After all floors are not just for standing on, I mean you can have the partial floor motif….

What Smithson found was that, to the architect, the floors of this demolished building were of little importance, they were 'trick-floors' which were meant only to trigger off an oscillating process of construction/destruction (architecturisation/de-architecturisation). It seemed to Smithson that this oscillating was more important to the architect than any actual edification of a functional architectural object. Buildings, in this sense, were a pretext for the circulation of the architect's drives. Pre-determined by a drive, to de-architecturise the hotel, the building was destined to undergo a man-made collapse in advance of a natural one.

Such scattering and breakdown was, for Smithson, the familiar face of entropy. Throughout the lecture, coupling itself with the architect's death drive, is Smithson's desire, seeking gratification through the recognition of entropy. Here entropy guaranteed the constancy of desire, the regular replenishing of the drives and the perpetual supply of the object of desire [object a].

Smithson was of the view that one of the primary functions of modernist architecture was to repress the Other with the weight of ideologies and idealisations. Such architecture was derided for its idealist aims of improving human conditions and its rhetoric of Universal man. What these buildings repressed, and Hotel Palenque did not, was a certain entropic material collapse inherent in the building from its origins. Throughout Smithson's slide lecture, the Hotel Palenque therefore served both as a pretext to set free the architect's drives as well as to quench Smithson's thirst for entropy.

de-, dis-, ex-.

After circulating through further rooms, to end the tour Smithson left the hotel, first by the front door and then by the back door. At the front entrance, the Other lurked peacefully enough; turtles were still swimming unhampered by crocodile companions. The old green wooden back door was more his exit, pulled closed by a mouth-like bar. Above this bar, two faded pieces of paper gave the impression of blank eyes. The whole door which "opens on nowhere and closes on nowhere" stood like a *vacant gaze*.

What so delighted Smithson was the way in which this homespun hotel inadvertently let slip something that he found very true. The architect's drive had produced all these rather absurd gazing points [objects a] in the building, all the dereliction and demolition, in pursuit of a pleasure never to be attained, though one day the completed edifice might momentarily give the illusion that it had. On entering the hotel the subject engaged in a fantasy relationship with architectural objects.

The *Hotel Palenque* lecture was a pedagogical event, in the sense that

Robert Smithson,
from *Hotel Palenque*
series, 1969.
Courtesy of
Jon Weber Gallery

it was a lesson about an encounter with an 'architectural unconscious'. By the time Smithson departed via the back door, the bemused architectural student had been given a greater sense of what it could mean to be a desiring subject when looking at architecture. For Smithson, this required looking at those places in which the 'architectural unconscious' had slipped through. What may have seemed at first to have been mundane builder's silly business, or even architectural stupidity, turned out to be worth far more attention than had been thought. Smithson's gaze, gratified by the tour of the Hotel Palenque, demonstrated how desire is capable of eroding traditional architectural limits denied through a systematic taming of entropy.

○

1. Stuart Morgan, 'An art against itself: Functions of Drawing in Robert Smithson's Work', *Arts Magazine*, May 1978, p. 125.
2. An introduction to Lacan's conception of the unconscious as 'Other' can be found in the first chapter of Bruce Fink, *The Lacanian Subject: Between Language and Jouissance*, Princeton University Press, 1995.
3. A particularly familiar Freudian example of this 'Other' voice can be found in slips of the tongue.
4. "Le désir de l'homme, c'est le désir de l'Autre." There are perhaps three translations of this in English: Man's desire is the same as the Other's desire; Man's desire is the desire for the Other, Man's desire is to be desired by the Other. Alternative translations can be found in Bruce Fink, op. cit., p. 54.
5. Virginia Dwan's account of this trip can be found in 'Reflections on Robert Smithson', *Art Journal*, Fall 1982, p. 233.
6. The draft article is 'Pointless Vanishing Points', *The Collected Writings of Robert Smithson*, University of California Press, Berkeley, 1996, p. 358, (hereafter *S2*); 'Interpolation of the Enantiomorphic Chambers' appeared in the Finch College exhibition catalogue, *Art in Process*, 1966, *S2*, p. 39. Drawings include *Afterthought Enantiomorphic Chambers, Drawing Y* and *Drawing Z*.
7. Nancy Holt and Peter Hutchinson recall them being parallel. The oblique arrangement described above differs from the parallel by about 2 radial degrees. It would have been easy to adjust it to either.
8. 'Pointless Vanishing Points', 1967, *S2*, p. 358.

de-, dis-, ex-.

9. Lacan indicated that the formation of the ego during the infant "mirror stage" arose from identification with one's own mirror image. Unlike the body, this image appears as unified. See 'The Mirror Stage as formative of the function of the I', *Ecrits*, Routledge, London, 1995, p. 1.

10. All of these texts were in Smithson's library with the exception of Derrida's *Of Grammatology*.

11. 'A Refutation of Historical Humanism', 1967, *S2*, p. 336.

12. In 'Pointless Vanishing Points' Smithson conflates one-point perspective and Cartesian space in the various survey techniques used in measuring and mapping land. Martin Jay discusses this as the scopic structure of the *Ancien Régime*, in *Downcast Eyes: The Denigration of Vision in Twentieth-Century Thought*, University of California Press, 1993.

13. Smithson's attack on Michael Fried in 'Letter to the Editor', *S2*, p. 66, concludes by considering "a subdivided progression of 'Frieds' on millions of stages."

14. 'Four Conversations between Dennis Wheeler and Robert Smithson', *S2*, p. 202.

15. The concept of "dedifferentiation" was based on Anton Ehrenzweig's *The Hidden Order of Art*, of 1967. This Freudian account of artistic practice was quite widely read among the minimalists, and was quoted by Robert Morris. Ehrenzweig's theorisation of artistic practice described three stages. First, was "an initial ('schizoid') stage of project-ing fragmented parts of the self into the work." In this phase, the unconscious projec-tions are felt as alien and even persecutory. The second dedifferentiated stage tended toward a manic oceanic limit where fragmentation was given coherence and, thirdly, re-introjected into the ego. See *The Hidden Order of Art*, Weidenfeld Press, pp. 102-105.

16. Smithson differs from Lacan in his emphasis on the two-eyed structure of vision, as based on the stereo optics of Wheatstone. Lacan's biologism was based on Roger Caillois' study *Mimicry and Legendary Psychasthenia*.

17. 'A Sedimentation of the Mind', 1968, *S2*, p. 107.

18. Ibid., p. 106.

19. Lacan: "It is here that I propose that the interest the subject takes in his own split is bound up with that which determines it - namely, a privileged object, which has emerged from primal separation, from self-mutilation induced by the very approach of the real, whose name, in our algebra, is the *objet a*." 'Anamorphosis', 'Of the Gaze as Objet Petit a', *The Four Fundamental Concepts of Psycho-analysis*, Penguin Books, 1977, p. 83. My use is thus a simplification of Lacan's theory. In fact, the split brings on three new factors, S1, S2, and [object a]. As I am particularly concerned with the scopic regis-ter and the relation $ (a, rather than the Symbolic, consideration of the chain of signi-fiers S1) S2 has been omitted.

20. 'A Sedimentation of the Mind', 1968, *S2*, p. 112.

21. 'Pointless Vanishing Points', 1967, *S2*, p. 358.

22. This comparison was brought to my attention by Michael Corris of Oxford-Brooks University

23. Jacques Lacan, 'Anamorphosis', *The Four Fundamentals of Psycho-analysis*, Penguin Books, 1994, p. 79.

24. Rosalind Krauss, 'A User's Guide to Entropy', *October*, No. 55, Fall 1996, p. 57.

25. A transcript of this lecture can be found in 'Insert Robert Smithson', *Parkett*, No. 43, 1995, pp. 117-132. The photographs with fragments of the lecture also appear in Robert Sobieszek, *Robert Smithson: Photo Works*, University of New Mexico Press, 1993.

26. 'Fragments of an Interview with P.A. Norvell', 1969, *S2*, p. 194. In this quote the materials function as an architectural [object a]: "...there is nothing like a pile of cement just as cement."

27. 'A Sedimentation of the Mind', 1968, *S2*, p.112.

Beatriz Colomina

Reflections on the Eames House

The oldest published photograph shows a truck on the site, occupying the place of the house, taking its place, anticipating it. The windshield happens to lie exactly where a glass facade will terminate the building. The steel frame of the house is being assembled from a crane on the back of the truck as it steadily moves down the narrow site carved out between a steep hillside and a row of eucalyptus trees. It is said that this process took only a day and a half.[1]

The Eameses immediately celebrated. A sequence of photographs shows the ecstatic couple holding hands under the frame, then stepping off the retaining wall on to a thin beam suspended like a tightrope across the space, and finally posing in the middle of the beam, still holding hands. Ray has a white bird in her raised hand.[2]

The Eameses liked to celebrate things. Anything. Everything. This is not just whimsy, a distraction from the work. It is part of the work itself. Walking along the beam of the house under construction is the beginning of the occupation of the house. They are literally moving in, even if the crafting of the basic fabric of the building was to take almost a year. The house became an endless process of celebration over the course of their lives.[3] When they walk across the steel tightrope before the tent has even been pulled up over the frame, they are launching an intense program of construction through festive play. Every stage of the play is recorded, photographed, and disseminated to an international audience.

The circus, it turns out, was one of the Eames' fascinations. So much so, that in the mid-1940s, out of work and money, they were about to audition as a clown act when a financial deal related to the production of their plywood furniture came.[4] And when in 1970 Charles was asked to give the prestigious Charles Eliot Norton

de-, dis-, ex-.

The *Eames House* under construction, 1949

Ray and Charles on the newly con-structed steel frame of their house

Lectures at Harvard University, he concluded the first of his six lec-tures by presenting a three-screen slide show of circus photographs he had been shooting since the 1940s. The 180 images were accom-panied by a sound-track featuring music and other sounds recorded at the circus. Eames turned to the circus because what "seems to be a freewheeling exchange in self-expression, is instead a tightly knit and masterfully disciplined organic accumulation of people, ener-gies and details."[5] In a talk given before the American Academy of Arts and Sciences in 1974, he elaborates on the point:

> The circus is a nomadic society which is very rich and
> colorful but which shows apparent license on the sur-
> face.... Everything in the circus is pushing the possible
> beyond the limit.... Yet, within this apparent free-
> wheeling license, we find a discipline which is almost
> unbelievable. There is a strict hierarchy of events and

an elimination of choice under stress, so that one event can automatically follow another. The layout of the circus under canvas is more like the plan of the Acropolis than anything else.[6]

In many ways, this is what Eames thought architecture was, the ongoing theatrical spectacle of everyday life, understood as an exercise in restrictions rather than self-expression. The endless photographs of the ridiculously happy Eameses displaying their latest inventions are part of an extraordinarily precise and professional design practice. We see them on top of the frame of their house, "pinned" by metal chair frames, holding Xmas decorations, waving to us from inside a Xmas ball, wearing Easter hats or masks, photographing their own reflections in the house, and so on. In almost all of the early photographs they wear matching outfits as if to emphasise the performative aspect of their work. The Eameses were very precise about their clothes, commissioning their dress from Dorothy Jenkins, the Oscar-winning designer who did the costumes for many films, including South Pacific, The Ten Commandments, Night of the Iguana, and The Sound of Music (Ray Eames' distinctive pinafore dresses are even reminiscent of Julie Andrews' dresses in this film). The effect of the Eames costume is of the professional couple as a matching set, carefully positioned like any other object in the layout. The uniform clothes transform the couple into a designer object that can be moved around the frame or from picture to picture. It is always the layout that is the statement, not the objects. And the layout is constantly reworked, rearranged.

If design is not the self-expression of the designer, it is the occupant's daily life that leaves its mark on the house. All the ephemera of daily living take over and define the space. In the Eames House, the real architecture was to be found in their endless rearrangement of collectables within it. The real space was to be found in the details of their daily life.

For the Eameses, everything is architecture, from the setting of a table for breakfast to a circus performance. Everybody is a designer. Employees arriving at the Eames Office were routinely assigned tasks for which they had no previous experience.[7] It was thought that anybody who applied his or her attention totally, obsessively, to a problem would come up with a good solution, especially if there were many restrictions, such as limited time, materials or money. Eames spoke nostalgically of his days at the MGM studios, where he often had only one night to make a whole new set out of a limited range of props.

This idea of design as the rearrangement of a limited kit of parts is constant in their work. Everything they produce can be rearranged, no layout is ever fixed. Even the formal lectures were sometimes rearranged in midstream. Kits of parts, movable partitions, "the Toy," the plywood cabinets, the House of Cards, the Revell toy house, the Kwikset House are all infinitely rearrangable.

The Eames House is a good example. Not only was it produced out of the same structural components as the utterly different Entenza House (designed by Charles Eames with Eero Saarinen), but the Eames House was itself a rearrangement of an earlier version. After the steel had already been delivered to the site, Eames decided to redesign the house. He put the same set of steel parts together in a completely new way.[8]

And it is not just the frame that gets rearranged. Rather than produce a complete, fixed, environment for the post-war consumer, the Eameses offered a variety of components with which individuals could construct and rearrange themselves. Their own house was the paradigm: panels shift, furniture moves in and out. The house became a kind of testing ground for all the work of the office. Everything moves in the end. Only the basic frame stays still and this frame is meant to be almost invisible. A necessary prop – no more than that. As Esther McCoy writes, as a caption for an image of trees reflected on the glass walls of the Eames House:

> After thirteen years of living in a house with an exposed
> steel frame, Ray Eames said, 'The structure long ago
> ceased to exist. I am not aware of it'. They lived in nature
> and its reflections – and reflections of reflections.[9]

The house dissolves itself in a play of reflections, restless images

Charles and Ray, pinned by chair
leg bases to a sidewalk,
photographed from the roof
of the Eames office

that immediately caught the eye of the world. The Eames House was published everywhere, exposed, scrutinised.[10] The images multiplied and became the objects of reflection. Their appeal was part of the general fascination with post-war America that extended from pop–up toasters to buildings.

Perhaps nobody was so captivated by the Eameses, and more lucid about their work, than their buddies the British architects Alison and Peter Smithson. In a 1966 AD issue devoted exclusively to the Eameses and prepared by the Smithsons, they wrote:

> There has been much reflection in England on the Eames House. For the Eames House was a cultural gift parcel received here at a particularly useful time. The bright wrapper has made most people – especially Americans – throw the content away as not sustaining. But we have been brooding on it – working on it – feeding from it.[11]

The house as an object, a gift all wrapped up in coloured paper. This comment reflects so much of the Smithsons' obsessions, so much of what they saw as new in the Eameses: the attention to seemingly marginal objects (which the Smithsons perceptively understood as "remnants of identity"), the love of ephemera, of coloured wrapping paper, and so on.

For the Eameses, gifts were all important. They maintained that the reason they began to design and make toys (the House of Cards, The Toy, the masks, etc) was to give them to their grandchildren and the children of staff members and friends. But the concept of gifts extends far beyond the toys. Not only were the Eameses extremely generous with their friends (they once paid for airline tickets so the Smithsons could visit them in California), but they understood all their work as a gift. In an interview Charles said: "The motivation behind most of the things we've done was either that we wanted them ourselves, or we wanted to give them to someone else. And the way to make that practical is to have the gifts manufactured.... The lounge chair, for example, was really done as a present to a friend, Billy Wilder, and has since been reproduced." Wilder wanted "something he could take a nap on in his office, but that wouldn't be mistaken for a casting couch."[12] In addition to the "nap" chair, the Eameses designed a "TV chair" for Wilder. An article in a 1950 issue of *Life* magazine shows a multiple exposure photograph of Billy Wilder moving back and forth on the plywood lounge chair of 1946, claiming that it was designed so that the "restless Wilder can easily jump around while watching television."

From the toys, to the furniture, to the houses (which were either designed for their closest friends, John Entenza and Billy Wilder, or as toys like the Revell House and the Birthday House designed for Hallmark Cards in 1959), to the major productions (such as the film Glimpses of the U.S.A., which they understood as a token of friendship to the Russians), to their most complex exhibitions, the Eameses always concentrated on what they were giving and how it should be presented. Everything was thought of as a gift. Design was gift-giving.

The sense of the Eames House as a gift also points to the constant shift in scale in their work: from house to cabinets, to children's furniture, to toys, to miniatures. Even the architectural models are treated like toys, played with by excited architects and clients acting like curious children. Eames once said that in the "world of toys he

Children in architecture (handwritten note)

Eames House, ca. 1952

saw an ideal attitude for approaching the problems of design, because the world of the child lacks self–consciousness and embarrassment."[13] In Eames' architecture everything is a toy, everybody is a child. Perhaps this explains the constant presence of children in the photographs of their work. Since when have we seen so many children in architecture?

Charles and Ray saw everything through the camera. They used to shoot everything. This was surely not just an obsession with recording. There is that, no doubt, but they also made decisions on the basis of what they saw through the lens, as is evident in Ray's description of the process of decision-making in the Eames House:

> We used to use photographs. We would cut out pieces

Reflections of trees on the glass facade of the
Eames House photographed by Charles

de-, dis-, ex-.

from photographs and put them onto a photograph of the house to see how different things would look. For instance – there was a space in the studio we wanted filled. It was between the depth of the floor where it opens for the stairs. We wondered what to do. We had some pier pylons from Venice pier (we had wanted to keep something of it to remember it by). Well, we had pictures of it, glued them onto a photo and decided it worked so we went ahead and did it.[14]

To remember the Venice pier they took a piece of it with them. This is characteristic of the Eameses who over the years accumulated an astonishing quantity of objects. The pylons can be seen standing outside the house. But to see if they could keep a memory of the object inside the house they used photographs and collage. Indeed, a photograph of the Venice pier ended up filling the space in the house they had tested using collage.

The photocollage method had already been important to architects of the early European avant–garde. Mies van der Rohe photocollages a drawing of the office building of 1919 onto a photograph of the Friedrichstrasse, glues photographs of landscape, materials and a Klee painting to the Resor House drawings, and glues together photographs of landscape, sculpture and paintings in the project of the Museum for a Small City. The structure of the building gives way to a juxtaposition of photographic images. But it would be important to understand in what sense the Eameses transformed the strategies of the avant-garde. How was the Eames House able to "trigger," in Peter Smithson's words, "a wholly different kind of conversation"?

The Smithsons wrote:

> In the 1950s the Eames moved design away from the
> machine aesthetic and bicycle technology, on which it
> had lived since the 1920s, into the world of the cine-
> ma–eye and the technology of the production aircraft;
> from the world of the painters into the world of the
> lay–out men.[15]

This shift from the machine aesthetic to colour film, from the world
of painting to that of the lay-out men, from Europe to California,
can be traced in the shift between the first and second versions of
the Eames House. The first version, the so–called Bridge House,
published in *Arts & Architecture* in 1945, seems to be based on Mies's
1934 sketch of a glass house on a hillside. The scheme was rejected
in 1947, after Charles went to MoMA to photograph the Mies exhibition, in which the sketch was first made public. Charles must have
already known. In fact, he said that he didn't see anything new in
the projects that were exhibited, but he was impressed by Mies's
design of the exhibition itself. Shortly after his visit to the exhibition, the Eameses came up with a new scheme for their house.

The first version, which Charles designed with Eero Saarinen, faith-
fully followed the Miesian paradigm in every detail. The house is
elevated off the ground as a kind of viewing platform. The sheer
glass walls are aimed at the landscape, lined up with the horizon. In
the original drawings, published in *Arts & Architecture* in December
1945, we see the occupant of the house standing behind the glass,
an isolated figure looking out at the world that is now framed by the
horizontal structure. The interior is almost empty. In the model of
the house published in March 1948, the only thing occupying the

de-, dis-, ex-.

Model of *Case Study House #8*, published in *Arts and Architecture*, March 1948

house is the reflection of the surrounding trees, which the Eameses went to considerable trouble to photograph by placing the model on the actual site, carefully superimposing an image of the trees in the foreground. The effect is classic Mies. As in the Farnsworth House, there is a stark elevated interior with at most a few isolated pieces of furniture floating near the glass in a fixed pattern prescribed by the architect.

In the second version the house is dropped to the ground and swung around to hug the hillside. It no longer faces the ocean. The view is now oblique and filtered by the row of eucalyptus trees in front of the long east face. A low wall is wrapped around the patio on the south facade, partially blocking the ocean from the view of someone sitting in the space and focusing attention on the patio as an extension of the house, as an interior. The dominant focus is now in rather than out. The house abandons the Miesian sandwich,

The *Eames House* living room with tatami mats, 1951

de-, dis-, ex-.

where floating slabs of floor and ceiling define a strictly horizontal view. The floor is treated like a wall with a series of frames defined by rugs, tiles, trays, and low tables on which objects are carefully arranged. In fact, floor, wall, and ceiling are treated in a similar way. Not only are they now given the same dimension (the sandwich being replaced by a box) but they start to share roles. Hans Hofmann paintings used to hang horizontally from the ceiling. Ray said that it was necessary to protect them from the strong light, and that they "would be able to see them well from that position."[16] Many photographs of the house are taken from a very low angle, and we often see the Eameses sitting on the floor surrounded by their objects. The west wall is clothed in birch because they needed something they could hang objects on. On the east wall, much of the glass has become translucent or is wired ("to make people realize it is there"[17]) or replaced with opaque coloured panels. The sheer surface is broken up with louvres. The occupants can only see fragments of the outside, fragments that have the same status as the objects that now take over the interior. The view is there but restricted to a few of the many frames. Everything overlaps, moves and changes. The singular unmediated view is replaced by a kaleidoscopic excess of objects.

The eye that organised the architecture of the historical avant–garde has been displaced by a multiplicity of zooming eyes. Not by chance, the Eames' 1955 film *House: After Five Years of Living* is made up entirely of thousands of slides. Every aspect of the house is scrutinised by these all–too–intimate eyes. The camera moves up close to every surface, every detail. But these are not the details of the building as such, they are the details of the everyday life that the building makes possible.

The film as a succession of slides is consistent with the house itself. It is impossible to focus in the Eames House in the same way that we do in a house of the 20s. Here the eye is that of a TV watcher. Not the 50s TV watcher but closer to that of today – multiple screens, some with captions, all viewed simultaneously. It helps to follow more than one story at once.

To some extent the Eameses pioneered this mode of viewing. They were experts in communication. In 1959 they brought *Glimpses of the USA* to Moscow, projecting it on the seven screens suspended within Buckminster Fuller's geodesic dome. 2,200 still and moving images presented the theme of "A Day in the Life of the United States." Fuller said that nobody had done it before and advertisers and film makers would soon follow.[18]

The Eames House is also a multiscreen performance. But Mies is not simply abandoned. Indeed, the house takes an aspect of Mies's work to its extreme. When Eames gave up on the first scheme after seeing the Mies exhibition at MoMA, he did so because he saw something else there. In fact, it was the exhibition technique that inspired him. When he published his photographs of the exhibition in *Arts & Architecture* he wrote: "The significant thing seems to be the way in which he has taken documents of his architecture and furniture and used them as elements in creating a space that says, 'this is what it is all about'."[19]

Eames was very impressed by the zooming and overlapping of scales: a huge photomural of a small pencil sketch alongside a chair towering over a model next to a twice–life–size photograph, and so on. He also noted the interaction between the perspective of the room and that of the life–sized photographs. The visitor experiences

de-, dis-, ex-.

Mies's architecture, rather than a representation of it, by walking through the display and watching others move. It is a sensual encounter: "The exhibition itself provides the smell and feel of what makes it, and Mies van der Rohe great."[20]

What Eames learned from Mies, then, was less about buildings, more about the arrangement of objects in space. Exhibition design, layout, and architecture were indistinguishable, as Mies had demonstrated in his layout for the magazine G, his numerous exhibitions with Lilly Reich, the Silk Cafe, the Barcelona Pavilion, and so on. Eames picked up on the idea that architecture was exhibition and developed it.

Once again, the Eames House takes something from history and transforms it. The house is an exhibition, a showroom, but it is a different kind of showroom from those of the modern movement. The multiple eye belongs to a completely different kind of consumer. It is the eye of the postwar acquisitive society. While Mies is famous for his comment "Less is more," the Eameses said that their "objective is the simple thing of getting the most of the best to the greatest number of people for the least."[21] The glass box gives way to such a density of objects that even the limits of the box are blurred. The role of the glass changes. With Mies, reflections consolidate the plane of the wall. The complex lines of trees become like the veins in marble. With the Eames House, the plane is broken. The reflections of the eucalyptus trees are endlessly multiplied and relocated. Eames even replaces a panel on the south facade with a photograph of a reflection of the trees, confirming that every panel is understood as a photographic frame.

The showroom quality of the Eames House is exemplified by its repeated use as the site of fashion photographs. Magazines like *Life* and *Vogue* insert their models into the building, lining them up with the architecture, even merging them into the interior elements. In this, the house participates in another long tradition of the histori- cal avant–garde. Ever since the turn of the century, modern archi- tecture has been used as a setting for fashion publicity. In fact, the history of modern architecture is the history of the showroom, the history of a blending of architecture and exhibition. But the Eames House is no longer just a uniform backdrop for fashion designs as discrete innovations. The garments are blended into the fabric of the house, mingling with the objects. The accompanying text bounces backwards and forwards between the "California bold look" of the architecture and the fashion. What is on display in the show- room is the equal status of all kinds of objects. The announcement of Case Study Houses #8 and #9 in the December 1945 issue of *Arts & Architecture* shows the silhouettes of both the Eameses and Entenza surrounded by the galaxy of objects that define their respective lifestyles. The role of the architect is simply that of hap- pily accommodating these objects.

Perhaps nowhere are the differences between Mies and Eames clear er than in the photographs of their houses under construction. A photograph of the Farnsworth House shows the lonely figure of Mies with his back to the camera sombrely appraising the empty frame. His enormous figure cuts a black silhouette into the frigid landscape. With his coat on, he stands like a Caspar David Friedrich figure confronting the sublime. At about the same time, but a world away, the Eameses put on their new outfits, climb into their frame, and smile at the camera.

1. The Eameses said that the structural shell of the House was raised by five men in 16 hours. 'Life in a Chinese Kit: Standard Industrial Products Assembled in a Spacious Wonderland', *Architectural Forum*, September 1950, p. 94.

2. The first one was published in *Blueprints for Modern Living*, 182, and credited to the Eames office. The second in 'Steel in the Meadow', *Interiors*, Nov. 1959, p.109, is attributed to Jay Connor. The third, reproduced here, was printed in John Neuhart, Marilyn Neuhart and Ray Eames, *Eames Design: The Work of the Office of Charles and Ray Eames*, Harry N. Abrams, 1989, p. 108. It is attributed to John Entenza.

3. Not by chance they moved into their house on the eve of Xmas 1949.

4. See Pat Kirkham, *Charles and Ray Eames: Designers of the Twentieth Century*, MIT Press, 1995, p. 150. See also Saul Pett, 'Charles Eames: Imagination Unlimited', *St. Louis Post–Dispatch*, July 27, 1971, p. 3.

5. '1970, Charles Eliot Norton Lectures: Lecture 1', *Eames Design*, p. 356.

6. *Bulletin of the American Academy of Arts and Sciences*, October 1974. Quoted in *Eames Design*, op. cit., p. 91.

7. Pat Kirkham, *Charles and Ray Eames*, op. cit., p. 89.

8. While many sources insist, following the Eameses, that the new version used only those parts already delivered to the site, with the exception of one additional beam, Marilyn and John Neuhart question it: "A count of the seventeen–foot vertical girders needed for both house and studio yields a total of twenty–two for the first and sixteen for the latter, considerably more than would have been needed for the first version of each. In addition, there do not appear to have been any seventeen–foot girders in the original house. Additional trusses would also have been required to accommodate the reworked plan." *Eames House*, Ernst & Sohn, 1994, p. 38.

9. Esther McCoy, *Case Study Houses 1945–1962*, Hennessey & Ingalls, 1977, p. 54. First published in 1962 under the title *Modern California Houses*.

10. In addition to *Arts and Architecture*, the Eames House was published in *Architectural Forum*, September 1950, *Architectural Review*, October 1951, *Arquitectura*, Mexico, June 1952, *L'Architecture d'aujourd'hui*, December 1953, *Interiors*, November 1959, *Domus*, May 1963, *Architectural Design*, September 1966, etc.

11. Alison and Peter Smithson, 'Eames Celebration', *Architectural Design*, Vol. XXXVI, September 1966, p. 432.

12. 'Q&A: Charles Eames by Digby Diehl', p. 17.

13. See 'Eames, Charles', *Entry in Current Biography* 1965, p. 142.

14. Ray Eames in an Interview with Pat Kirkham, July 1983. Manuscript in the Library of Congress.

15. Peter Smithson, 'Just a Few Chairs and a House: An Essay on the Eames–Aesthetic', *Architectural Design*, September 1966, p. 443.

16. "We hung them off the ceiling for two reasons – one was because they needed to be kept away from strong light and the second was because we thought we would be able to see them well from that position." Ray Eames in Interview with Pat Kirkham, July 1983. Transcript in the Library of Congress.

17. Charles Eames quoted in 'Life in a Chinese Kit: Standard Industrial Products Assembled in a Spacious Wonderland', *Architectural Forum*, September 1950.

18. Letter from Buckminster Fuller to Ms. Camp, November 7, 1973. Eames Archives, Library of Congress.

19. Charles Eames, 'Mies van der Rohe', photographs by Charles Eames taken at the exhibition, *Arts & Architecture*, December 1947, p.27.

20. Ibid.

21. *TIME*, July 10, 1950.

Howard Caygill

See Naples
and Die

...a scintillating light whose very flash consists in extinguishing itself, a light which at the same time is and is not.

Emmanuel Levinas

Obliteration

What Levinas says of obliteration holds more for photography than for sculpture. To paraphrase 'Reality and its Shadow' (1948) – the photograph obliterates its object by marking its removal; it is as though the photographed object "died, were degraded, were disincarnated in its own reflection." The light at the moment of exposure is ubiquitous in the photograph – it is the photograph – yet only as reflected off the objects and actions that make up the shot. The light is once obliterated by its reflection off objects and then again by its technological translation into a photograph.

What prevents obliteration becoming another name for Platonic participation? Its operation seems to be governed by the same philosophical syntax: the light of the idea is broadcast by imitation first in things and then through the mimetic work of art. The difference between obliteration and participation lies in their relation to time – both work with the collateral of eternity, but in participation the eternal idea is the source of light, while for obliteration it is the enduring light which is the source of eternity. The photographed light has already passed, it is elsewhere; while the photograph endures in its wake, part of another pattern of light moving through and past us.

Obliteration is not annihilation, not the simple inversion of Platonism which would urge absence and nothingness in the place of presence and plenitude. It stamps a moment, at once realising it and giving it a term. I obliterated my railway ticket at Roma Termini before boarding the train for Naples by stamping it in a golden box. It was marked with time and place and some numbers of occult significance, all of which allowed the journey to begin, but at the cost of announcing its end. Obliteration is in one respect deferred destruction – an envelope of future determined in advance – but in another it marks the possibility of a future, of an arrival in Naples. Even when taken to the limit cases of the infinitesimally small and the infinitely long journeys, the obliterated ticket still marks a delay and a promise, a sign of endurance. Unlike the Platonic return journey of participation, which moves irresistibly from idea to appearance and back to idea, obliteration marks a hiatus or caesura which is not always traversible – the promised arrival does not always happen.

Levinas saw the enduring interval as monstrous and inhuman, but it can also mark risk. Obliteration does not guarantee arrival, but only the possibility of the journey. The melancholy question of how many photographs were never seen, are seen no more, or are yet to be seen, only makes sense within a Platonic aesthetic in which the moment of participation is fallen and in need of redemption. The photograph is a return ticket that captures the light of the idea participated in objects and then through the abstraction, approximates them to the original idea – the truth of the eternal in the momentary. The photograph understood as an obliteration of an obliteration simply marks the moment at which a journey was recommenced – when the light passed by – there is no return, and its recapitulation in the photograph makes little difference.

Can this condition of photography be achieved – is it possible to

achieve a photograph that does not yield the Barthian affect of nostalgia? Probably not, since intention however removed, always intrudes. Even when trying to enact a programme of negative photography – stripping away to the degree zero of a disposable camera – walking blindfold randomly exposing the film at fixed intervals – taking superfluous photographs which did not need to be seen, the act remains replete with meaning. Spatial and chromatic organisation is built into the technology, the tourist gaze encoded in the random and blind wandering, a retrospective significance applied to the insignificant, a few moments in Naples on the morning of September 9, 1997 ineptly redeemed. But maybe this is too parochial – one day photographs will die and lose their meaning. The seemingly infinite heap of photographs will shrivel to nothing, human photography will be nothing but the family album of a line without heirs, thrown on the fire.

Shortly before his death in Naples in 1836, Leopardi wrote *La ginestra*, a poem to the broom which grew in the inhospitable soil of Vesuvius. Prefaced by John III, "And men loved darkness rather than the light" – it sees darkness in the eternal and light in the transient. The image of Pompeii emerging from the excavations is the negative of the image of human progress and mastery that characterised the "proud but foolish century" – the flames of exterminating Vesuvius destroying the city have become flickers in the memory, an object of curiosity for the tourist. Before the light of the stars and the nebulae, Leopardi wondered how our light will appear to them; perhaps this would be the light in which to look at photographs?

Exposure

I heard something else when the newsreader said "l'omicidio e lega-

to alla camorra" – "the murder is related to the camorra." The year of photography and the electronic image had arrived early with a spate of camera-related deaths. The most prominent act of terminal over–exposure was Princess Diana, the Saturday night/Sunday morning before my journey. Finally they owned the fantasy of murder by camera and the premiss that the camera is a weapon. From within the thwarted desire to see the shots of the crash emerged the fascination with the phantasmal photo–motorcyclist. The motorcyclist who they say overtook the Mercedes at high speed and popped the flash in the eyes of the driver, causing him to swerve and crash. Did the final photos of the slower paparazzi capture the assassins' flash, and was this the reason for their not being seen?

For a moment the camera was revealed as a weapon, not indirectly through its evidentiary effect, but directly as an instrument of murder: Le Monde carried a cartoon of the late Princess treading gingerly through a minefield of cameras. The death also opened a juridical dimension to the work of photographic obliteration. If the killer-photographer was a paparazzi, then the ultimate photograph of Princess Diana would be obliterated; it could never be seen without incriminating its author in the act of murder. Not the obliteration of camera and image, as in the photos taken by Cruise missiles which blank out the moment of obliteration, but the juridical obliteration of the image. The photograph would expose the photographer and testify to a presence at the scene and impute an intention. Perhaps every photograph should be given the same forensic scrutiny that would be accorded this final photograph?

Fun Camera

With few exceptions, the photograph pretends to the image and provokes theoretical narratives of mimesis and representation. Yet the drawing of passing light not only describes what appears in a given lit space but also draws the moment. The sense of the passing moment saturates even the most banal photograph and invites the melancholy discourse on photography as a work of mourning. A morning in Naples gone forever, a moment not seen but photographed and looked over later. Not this though, not the substitution of time for space, but something else; the taking of this passing light at this moment, the intersection of chance and necessity.

For Plato's account of photography forget *The Republic* and its cave of images and look instead to the themes of chance, necessity and technics proposed by the Athenian in Books IV and X of *The Laws*. Between the propositions that "human history is all an affair of chance" (709b) and "God sets the whole course of life for us" (709c) there is only technics. Adding to Plato's arts of "navigation, medicine and strategy" the techne of photography might pose the drawing of light as a powerful technology for propitiating chance and necessity. As with all techne, the risk of hubris is ineluctable; it is possible for techne to forget that it too is subject to chance and necessity, that this finitude is built into it. The products of this technology are as "perishable as their creators" but aspire to permanence; the technology itself aspires to overcome chance and necessity in omniscience. Poised between chance and necessity, technics cannot avoid obliteration however much it tries. Hence the hubris of the progressive histories of photographic technology which culminate, for now, in the digital camera and its reduction of chance and necessity to digital manipulation.

One way to propitiate chance and necessity would be to acknowledge their rule at the heart of the technology – to stress the limits of photographic technology. The obvious strategy is through the inten-

de-, dis-, ex-.

sification of hubris – the use of the digital camera and treatment of images – an option with the advantage of corporate sponsorship from Canon but with the risk of deferring the inevitable collision of chance and necessity. The inverse of this hyperstrategy would be to reduce the technology to its minimum, to photograph with an already obliterated technology, to choose the most abject means to draw the light.

I bought my throwaway cameras in an *edicola* in Roma Termini – there was not much time because the train was due to leave but then there was not much choice either. Instead of the long hours selecting lens and filters, a quick decision between four *Fun Cameras*: 'Classic', 'Flash', 'Panoramic' and 'Aqua–Sport'. They hang on carefully designed racks like packets of sweets at the supermarket checkout, their orange, purple and red packaging slightly tarnished by the sense of the end of another season. They appear the perfect commodity, promising "easy, worry-free picture taking"; I pay the 50,000 lira and take away the 'Classic' and the 'Panoramic'. Each is an individual carrying its own mark of obliteration in a serial number incorporating the life span of the camera – the 'Panoramic' is number 02/1999 262A and the 'Classic' 2938 04/99.

In a sense, these finite cameras perform the commodified obliteration of chance and necessity. With them nothing is left to chance – every snap obeys the brutal necessity of supplying an image – there is no control beyond pointing the camera, pushing the exposure button and winding on the film. And yet this almost complete submission to necessity promises a high exposure to chance. Intention is minimised in the name of ease and absence of worry; what the camera takes is beyond the control of the user. Added to this is the clumsiness of the technology – 'Classic' fits in the hand like an espi-

onage camera from a 60s movie, but it is difficult to find and engage the button; there is always the chance that the light has moved on before the film is exposed. The 'Panoramic' is an awkward rectangular box, an Odradek of a camera, indiscreet and almost impossible to hold in one hand; the click of the shutter is dull and mechanical and leaves little satisfaction. Winding on too is stiff, with hardly any indication that the next exposure has been reached.

The body of the camera is indistinguishable from its packaging which blazons melancholy scenes of family holidays and the Manhattan skyline; the only alleviation comes with the hope of technical incompetence – the chance that something might come out wrong or not at all. Otherwise this technology is structurally resentful, aimed at stopping movement, producing trophies for private family museums – although the camera itself is abandoned.

The bounds of necessity seem inescapable: Naples is one of the most looked-at cities in the world and hence one of the most spectral: the grand panoramic scenes of the Bay, Vesuvius, the Islands; the small genre scenes of everyday city life. I remember the diverse viewpoints of Micco Spadaro's *Eruption of Vesuvius* and Mattia Preti's *Three Children in a Scene of Charity* and look at my 'Panoramic' and 'Classic' cameras. The technology itself is haunted by the structure of the grand tourist's gaze – the 'Panoramic' for broad cityscape, the 'Classic' for the small genre scenes. Even the shape of the lens is programmed by the spectre of Naples. Can all this necessity be turned against itself?

The equipment became familiar as I walked unseeing through the city. After some exposures I learned to distinguish between the front and back of the camera and to find the exposure button. But it

was never automatic, and the limits of the technology ensured that photographic control was minimised. I did not know if I had taken any photographs. No fear of hubris, just the possible satisfaction that this was a technology which in aspiring to overcome chance made itself vulnerable to it.

Flaneurs

...anyone who is blind to forms sees little here.

Walter Benjamin and Asja Lacis

I like the moments in Walter Benjamin's *Arcades* Project when he leaves the well-beaten track that runs between the Louvre, Palais Royal and the Bibliothèque Nationale and finds himself wheezing up Rue Notre–Dame de Lorette or languishing in the 19th Arrondissement at Place du Maroc. Otherwise it is disappointing to realise that his Paris is geographically limited and that he very rarely practises the art of losing himself in the city. He comes closer to describing the terror of being disoriented in the city in his reminiscences of a Berlin childhood or of his bleak winter in Moscow. Similarly, he never loses himself in Naples, but takes careful and well–posed panoramic and genre shots while walking the established tourist routes.

Breaking all the rules of his own method, Benjamin seems to look so hard and intently that he does not get to see Naples. In spite of recommending the oblique view, the decisive blow struck with the left hand, he did not see the necessity of inverting the motto – "see Naples and die" – into "to see Naples it is necessary to die" – to not be present, to join the spectres. His text 'Naples' (1924) is a magnificent fraud – arriving at the Molo Beverello in the ferry from Capri he

walks with Asja Lacis towards the city centre, wanders around the Spanish Quarter, takes a ride in the funicular railway and then back to the ferry. In the text this stroll is carefully concealed by dissolving the topography of Naples into social and architectural porosity, with few clues about where they were to be found at any particular moment. In this famous evocation of the concrete experience of the city, the picture of Naples appears as a turn-of-the-century postcard – bright but out of focus.

The artistry of the essay lies in the way its authors manage to keep their cameras hidden and to cover their tracks. In the first five paragraphs – amid evocations of the Church, the camorra and the ill–fated congress of philosophers – they mention only one place – the hospital of San Gennaro which they visited for the catacombs. In order to evoke the city as a whole they pan through a view beginning from the ferry approaching port to one from above, from the Castell San Martino, producing an indistinct, grey panoramic blur. After this vertiginous shot, their gaze returns to the ferry and the approaching quayside of hotel and warehouse buildings, and then into the "anarchic village–like centre of the city."

Benjamin and Lacis give the impression of visiting the Neapolitan churches, but instead of describing them reflect on how they are impossible to find. Their quick description of stepped alleys and the life on the steps locates them in the Spanish Quarter, near the station of the funicular railway which they took to Castell San Martino. The most obvious route from Molo Beverello to the Spanish Quarter is along the Via Toledo, named and described by Benjamin and Lacis as "one of the busiest streets" and the scene of two paragraphs of picturesque description (as if taken with the 'Classic') supplemented by some reminiscences of the harbour district which they saw on

their way from the ferry. The mention of the festive character of Neapolitan life leads into a description of Sunday afternoon in Naples and some generic copy from the Baedecker guidebook about the firework displays of the Amalfi coast. They were also there on a Saturday, describing the draw of the lottery and, again, the hustle of the Via Toledo.

An exception to the absence of topography from the intense descriptions is the paragraph on the Arcades of Naples. Not the grandiose Galleria Umberto, but an arcade near the Spanish Quarter that is little more than a covered alley, but long enough to pose a challenge to anyone who would walk through and not fall "prey to the devil." Here begins the Arcades Project, an inauguration in which even the adversary of the Paris Arcades – the Department store – is neutralised. Leaving the arcade, Benjamin and Lacis find themselves again in the lower reaches of the Spanish quarter and take some snapshots of the housing and cafes that spill out onto the narrow streets and alleyways.

In terms of Neapolitan topography, Benjamin and Lacis' descriptions are drawn from a walk of less than an hour from the ferry port. Their snaps of Naples are contrived and vague, leaving the impression that they were trying to establish an alibi for the readers of the *Frankfurter Zeitung*. But perhaps they were elsewhere, refusing the melancholy choice between seeing the city and dying or dying and seeing the city. True to their guiding proposition – "everything joyful is mobile" – they interpret the Neapolitan's advice *"Vedere Napoli e poi Mori"* as "see Naples and then go on to Mori."

Shots
Beyond the dangers of the Neapolitan traffic there is the danger of

walking without sight but with cameras through a city under military occupation. In the face of an escalating series of camorra assassinations the Italian state ordered the military onto the streets of Naples. Images of soldiers in armoured cars driving through the city recall Belfast, and challenge the relaxed legality of the Neapolitans. The prime target is the horde of motor scooters, the means of transport preferred by the camorra assassins. They drive by and shoot into the crowd hoping to hit the target, usually a younger member of a rival family. With the arrest of the senior camorristi war has broken out between gionta and the gallo factions. But there are other means of camorra assassination, such as emerging from a crowded alley, attacking with a knife and then disappearing into the crowd. Understandably, the public, the camorra and the military are nervous of anyone walking around suspiciously reaching into their pockets.

The shouts of taxi–drivers touting for business, the roar of a plane flying low, broken glass underfoot and a child crying "mama." I hear and smell buses revving and feel the heat on my face and shoulders. Someone touches me saying "Signor, Signor" but I am unsure whether they are begging or helping. I have no problem with crossing roads, the traffic loops expertly around the pedestrian, as usual. At each quarter of an hour I nervously produce the cameras and quickly take a picture. I become sensitive to the paving stones, and hear someone telling me to go no further. Then later at the Piazza Plebiscito, the cameras spent, I look towards Vesuvius and catch sight of three small boys playing camorristi with toy revolvers and wish there was film left to take a shot. Later, looking at the random photograph of three boys with cameras I realise the lost photograph had already been taken.

de-, dis-, ex-.

Hal Foster

Trauma Studies and the Interdisciplinary

An interview

Alex Coles: With regard to your ongoing commitment to current critical art practice, how and why did the book on surrealism, Compulsive Beauty, *come about?*

Hal Foster: I have always wanted to work in the space between contemporary interests and historical concerns. I don't think one can do very incisive historical work without an optic of the present somehow in play. In relation to surrealism in particular, contemporary art and theory brought it into focus, in two or three different ways. Take subjectivity and sexuality: if one thought about these contemporary concerns historically, one had to deal with surrealism as a precedent. It was surrealism that first put psychoanalysis into play in modernist art. This was problematic. In terms of method, the art was often illustrational, but also in terms of sexual politics, it was often an acting out of mysogynistic fantasies. Nevertheless, the engagement begins there. Obviously, another surrealism has also come to the fore over the last decade, the surrealism of Bataille, a surrealism concerned less with desire than with abjection. That, too, has a resonance in contemporary art.

So there are two things: one general, which is that historical work needs the edge of contemporary commitment; and another more specific, that there was pressure to re-think surrealism. Now surrealism no longer has this dissident status in modernist studies, it is no longer neglected. Even its subversive status is not sure; in a way it has become an official model. I think we have to think otherwise, both for the present and in historical work.

AC: While the recovery of surrealism has been of great importance to contemporary work, do you think that it is now being over-privileged? Is this, dare I say it, not just a swing of the pendulum, away from a concern with

de-, dis-, ex-.

'mainstream modernism' to an 'alternative modernism'? Furthermore, do you think that the more recent shifts towards 'trauma culture' that you have outlined in your work, indicate a move away from surrealism?

HF: Surrealism has not become normative, but it is no longer subversive of our ideas of modernism. I, too, hesitate to see things in terms of simple alternation. Contemporary practices do not swing with the automatic movement of a pendulum. There are all kinds of doublings, reversals, spirals - it is a very complicated movement. Often past moments are recovered for present use, sometimes opportunistically, sometimes critically. One of the critical tasks of *The Return of the Real* was to develop a model with which to distinguish and to evaluate these different returns.

You suggest there is a shift away from this interest in surrealism to an interest in the traumatic. I see them as related, though the surrealist interest constitutes a problematic while the traumatic interest is a more general cultural syndrome, at least in America; it has all kinds of manifestations which need to be sorted out; some problematic, some provocative. In art there is a cluster of ideas about the abject, the obscene, and the traumatic. In part this is a reaction to a prior moment of postmodernist art and theory that proposed that the world was all image, that subjectivity was all surface. One reason for the violated bodies and nasty remainders in recent work is to insist that not everything is a sign, that not everything floats like a signifier, there are pre-symbolic residues. Sometimes this insistence is adolescent if not quite infantile in its desire to get outside the symbolic and the social. I do see it as mostly reactive. But I think there is a continuity between the recovery of surrealism and this interest in the traumatic.

AC: Would you say, for example, that Cindy Sherman's practice traces that history from the work in the late 1970s, to the work in the late 1980s?

HF: Sherman does the most to clarify this passage in art. It is not programmatic on her part (she is not indebted to theory) but in *The Return of the Real* I trace her work along Lacanian lines, in terms of concerns first with the feminine subject under the gaze of others, and then with the impossible position of the gaze of the world, with the obscene object of the real. I think her recent work expresses a pervasive revulsion against the image. This is evident in the way that it wants to break down the very frame of re-presentation, to force us right into a visual field that is dazzled into smithereens. The trajectory of her work shows these different interests at these different times, but that's obviously very schematic. She is not the only one by any means, but this is an argument I make in *The Return of the Real*.

AC: Just to take you back briefly to the idea of 'trauma studies', am I right to say that there is a problematic division that has been made between 'high' and 'low' versions of trauma discourse? That is, between art forms and 'reality shows', such as Oprah Winfrey's for instance?

HF: In fact this interest in traumatic subjectivity cuts across high and low. Subjectivity is understood as a matter of trauma on the talk show too, which leads to this paradoxical spectacle of confessions from people who are shattered, with no 'I' to confess. But this is also a privileged discourse of 'high' theory - disturbed subjectivity, traumatic history, and so on. So trauma discourse is quite general to the culture of this time - again, at least in America.

AC: With the integration of psychoanalysis - and specifically with the

de-, dis-, ex-.

Cindy Sherman, *Untitled Film Still, #7*, 1978 (detail). Courtesy the artist and Metro Pictures

arrival of the school of Lacanian theorists on the scene of art making - can we intimate that in fact interdisciplinarity is the European version of Trauma Studies?

Cindy Sherman,
Untitled #239, 1987.
Courtesy the artist
and Metro Pictures

HF: Recent uses of Lacan to think about Hollywood, popular culture and whatever, seems to me to constitute a high form of cultural studies (I mean in the American sense). Lacan interprets Hitchcock, Hitchcock illustrates Lacan; Nietzsche and telephones, Heidegger and e-mail - and so on. It is often incisive, often fun, but it is often very trivial too. Often the 'high' and 'low' terms remain very much in place; little disturbance of either term occcurs. So I am not sure what cultural-political work it actually does. At its worst it is 'Lacan for Beginners' for people who would rather go to the movies.

AC: Some of your most revealing insights regarding the politics of interdisciplinarity are planted in your footnotes, for example a footnote to your chapter 'The Artist as Ethnographer' in The Return of the Real *reads:*

de-, dis-, ex-.

"[interdisciplinary] exchanges are not trivial at a time when enrolments are counted closely - and when some administrators advocate a return to old disciplines, while others seek to recoup interdisciplinary ventures as cost-effective programs. Incidentally, these exchanges seemed governed by a used-car principle of discourse: when one discipline wears out a para-digm...it trades it in, it passes it on." Do you consider the métier of the art critic as necessarily interdisciplinary? Could you unpack the quote a little?

HF: The status of the interdisciplinary has changed over the last decade. Although I remain committed to it in principle, there are clearly problems. Even two decades ago there were very restrictive disciplinary conventions: nothing but disciplinary cops! This is not the case now. Today so much work that purports to be interdiscipli-nary seems to be non-disciplinary to me. To be interdisciplinary you need to be disciplinary first - to be grounded in one discipline, preferably two, to know the historicity of these discourses before you test them against each other. Many young people now come to interdisciplinary work before they come to disciplinary work. As a result they often fall into an eclecticism that does little work on any discipline; it is more entropic than transgressive. As for the foot-note, interdisciplinarity can be recouped institutionally as a cost-effective measure, to get fewer people to do more work. Do we really want departments of literature, art, art history, architecture, archi-tectural history, and film to be absorbed into one monster called Media Studies? I don't. But then all these matters develop unevenly; the politics are site-specific.

This is linked to the chapter called 'The Artist as Ethnographer' in *The Return of the Real.* Many artists and critics operate with a flat idea of culture now, and I wonder about its effects on practice. In the States there is an imperative to teach cultural forms of very different sorts as equal; it is one version of our pseudo-egalitarianism. As a result, the field of art is very hard to define. In some ways this is good and in some ways bad. Art needs structure, it needs constraint - enough resistance to articulate complicated thoughts and feelings. Right now, with this expanded idea of culture, art often seems arbitrary in its forms, ad-hoc in its engagements. I sometimes wonder what counts as expertise, what counts as history.

AC: *I get the sense that in the introduction to* The Return of the Real *you are picking up on something you intimate in the 1980s in 'Against Pluralism', namely, that there is the danger of a loss of critical awareness when one moves away from the notion of discipline. For instance, you write about certain artists being "footloose and fancy free"...or something like this.*

HF: There are progressive dimensions to tradition too. Think of Walter Benjamin - you are interested in him - it is a point he makes well: there are different forces, even revolutionary ones perhaps, in tradition. Tradition is never singular, especially not today. But in its complication it should not be dispersed. There are also resources in tradition that should not be simply cancelled in an avant-gardist gesture.

These issues are very much on the table now: what counts as tradition, what counts as memory, how important is a sense of the historicity of your practice? I am conservative enough to think that artists must elaborate the forms that they adopt through a critical reading of previous practices. I don't mean this in a Wölfflinian way - that each generation presents a problem which the next generation must somehow solve - but I do think there is a dialectic in advanced art, and that one pretends to escape it at the price of irrelevance.

[handwritten margin note:] or Y. A. Bois Painting As Model?

de-, dis-, ex-.

AC: *In* The Return of the Real, *there seems to be an increasingly evident tendency to affirm the necessity of the reconnection with what you name the diachronic axis of art practice and criticism by current moments. In the introduction you characterise this as the necessity of the present (synchronic) moment to act as a working through of previous diachronic moments or at least you address the necessity to keep the two axes in tension - in "critical co-ordination."*

HF: What I wanted to do in *The Return of the Real*, particularly in 'Who's Afraid of the Neo-Avant-Garde?', was not to reinstate a singular line of avant-garde practice but to claim that new ideas of temporality and narrativity are at work. The situation is not just one of lateral moves. In fact, one has an infinite number of options. What I mean by this is that I think that serious work does develop in one way or another the serious work that precedes it. But that's not to suggest that it is causal. In fact, my argument about the neo-avant-garde is that its temporality is complicated. For instance, it can run in reverse too. Maybe this is an old idea that goes back at least as far as T.S. Eliot, if not further. But I don't mean it in the way an Eliotic tradition does, that is to reinstate tradition. What I mean to suggest is that there are exchanges and relays between the past and the present that cannot be charted simply in terms of style and form. The relation is one of continual displacement, revision, and subsumption. But I do insist, and I think this is an important shift within my own work, that for all kinds of reasons we need models of historical connection as well as of historical rupture.

AC: *Some of these models you are developing seem to be based on psychoanalytic theories of the subject.*

HF: Right. This is one place where I am stimulated by the idea of trauma - in the more specific sense of another model of temporality where events do not happen punctually, where cause and effect are not immediate, where first moments are never simply originary and second moments never simply repetitive. This is my idea of how the avant-garde has developed over the century: later moments reposition prior moments; in a sense the avant-garde arrives from the future. In this way I have adapted the concept of "deferred action" in Freud. However, even as I pose the analogy I wonder about its validity: can one apply a model based on the subject to historical questions? It is a very common practice; perhaps all our models, not only of history but of the aesthetic, are secretly models of the subject.

which Freud text?

AC: *It seems to me that there is a commitment throughout your work to understand temporality in relation to various art forms and art works, that the gesture an artwork appears to be making can change throughout its life. You come across as strongly against types of art historical and critical work which arrest their objects within atemporal structures. In other words, you seem to be concerned to illuminate the fact that art works have a trajectory of their own within time.*

HF: That's right. Take the notion of recuperation, the notion that, in the end, the fate of all provocative practice is to be cancelled institutionally. There is a fatalism to this notion that disturbs me. Yet obviously it is important to think about the changed status of an object, of a practice in time, in particular in its reception by other practices. The genealogy of art is not a critical or historical imposition; it is worked out, in the first instance, by artists.

AC: *That takes us to the notion of genealogy and critical practices. In the postscript of 'Re: Post' (1984), after explaining the various critical approaches adopted by the current North American postmodern artists, you state*

de-, dis-, ex-.

that possibly the new imperative is to "think beyond the limits of critique." However, in the more recent 'Who's Afraid of the Neo-Avant-Garde?' (1994), you trace what you characterise as the causal self-critical chain of the avant-garde, positing artists such as Mark Dion, Fred Wilson and Andrea Fraser, as continuing a "deconstructive testing of the institution of art" (i.e., each further moment of the avant-garde is precisely to be understood as causally related to its precedent). Have your views shifted then? Or is the type of critique forwarded by these latter artists very different from the one you used to speak of, and posit as limiting, in the 1980s?

HF: Sometimes I am accused of historicism, but I am interested in genealogy, which is not a matter of simple causality. As for critique, there are only so many models on the left - Gramsci, the Frankfurt School, the Althusserian tradition. These remain important. But 'ideology-critique' or 'myth-critique' can become a doxa - an expression of contempt rather than of critique. It can also devolve into 'cynical reason', which is what I suggest in *The Return of the Real*. By the mid-1980s 'myth-critique' had degenerated into a situation where many artists had it both ways: a pretence of critique and a market style in one.

AC: Is this the kind of practitioner you used to characterise as a 'double agent'?

HF: No, there is a difference between cynical reason and critical ambivalence - the avant-garde as 'double agent'. The model there is Baudelaire, a figure who was able to turn socio-political ambivalence into creative criticality. To be a "double agent" is not necessarily to be complicit with both sides. One can be at work on both sides against both sides.

There is a fatigue now with our super-egos of critique. Often this is part of other reactions of an anti-intellectual, anti-theoretical, anti-political nature. But for many serious people, too, there is a fatigue with official notions of critique, especially ones that seem fatalistic. Certain positions in 'ideology-critique' like to proclaim the end of things: one wins if one declares *fini* to practice. 'Ideology-critique' does privilege the critic as final judge. I think critique should work to open up fields, not close them down.

AC: For a moment, can I just turn your attention specifically to the discussion of art and architecture? In the 1980s you seemed to have an interest in architectural practice and its criticism. Particularly, you seemed to have an interest in how similar divisions could be made in the architectural field as could be made in the artistic one. (I am thinking particularly about your discussion in 'Postmodern Polemics' [1985] of historicist postmodern practices, such as Michael Graves' and David Salle's, and poststructural practices, such as Peter Eisenman's and Laurie Anderson's.) Since then you seem to have written very little about architecture. Why is this?

HF: True, I was interested in architecture in the 1980s; if you were involved with debates about postmodernism you had to be. Unfortunately, people like Charles Jenks seized the term 'postmodernism' in the late 1970s in a very reductive way. It became a stylistic marker whereby postmodernism was really another term for anti-modernism. One necessary move was to wrestle the term away from this reductive use, to counter this anti-modernist idea of architecture with other ideas of what postmodernist architecture could be. Architecture and art are not as closely related now as they were then; architecture no longer has such a seminal importance in these debates.

AC: Let me just push you on one more thing. As the most recent precedent within the genealogy of avant-garde practice (which you trace in 'Who's Afraid of the Neo-Avant-Garde?') you cite the paradigm of the 'artist as ethnographer', represented by artists such as Mark Dion and Fred Wilson. I am wondering whether there are any more contemporary practices that you are interested in?

HF: Yes, there are. I mention Wilson and Dion in relation to one genealogy only. In many ways we are in a post-medium age, and so one question, now that the transgression of the mediums is tired, becomes, 'what counts as artistic structure; what constitutes the aesthetic field'? Practitioners in art, architecture, fiction, film - practitioners across the board - have begun to ask 'what might serve as a medium in a post-medium age'? These questions to do with specificity, autonomy, totality, seem very old but they have come back in new ways.

What counts as an image now; what serves as its material support, its structure; what is an image now technologically; is it photographic, indexical, digital? If images are digital, they can be archivally manipulated; there is a whole different sense of time in such images. The paradigm of the image for my kids, for instance, is the computer screen. It is an image that emanates from within; it is not projected; the montage is internal. So our basic ideas of representation are in mutation.

This renewed interest in the image, in the pictorial, comes as a surprise. So much art that has concerned me over the last three decades attacked the pictorial. But the pictorial has come back with a changed status that interests me now.

The Slade School of Fine Art

offers the following full-time courses:

BA (Hons) in Fine Art
MA in Fine Art
MFA in Fine Art
Graduate Diploma in Fine Art
MPhil/PhD in Fine Art
Affiliate Courses in Fine Art

for a prospectus and application details please contact:

The Slade School Administrator (Admissions), The Slade School of Fine Art,
University College London, Gower Street, London, WC1E 6BT

tel: +44 (0) 171 504 2313 fax: + 44 (0) 171 380 7801
e.mail: slade.enquiries@ucl.ac.uk http://www.ucl.ac.uk/slade/

Pursuing Excellence in Education and Research

UCL

byam shaw
SCHOOL OF ART

BA (Hons) Fine Art
Foundation and Diploma Studies
Post-graduate and
Short-term Studies

For further information on all
courses please contact:
The Academic Secretary
Byam Shaw School of Art
2 Elthorne Road Archway N19 4AG
Telephone 0171-281 4111
Fax 0171-281 1632
Email info@byam-shaw.ac.uk
Website http://www.byam-shaw.ac.uk

Goldsmiths
UNIVERSITY
OF LONDON

DEPARTMENT OF HISTORICAL
AND CULTURAL STUDIES

Angelus novus, 1920, Paul Klee. ©DACS 1997

For further details please contact:

The Secretary

Department of Historical and Cultural Studies

Goldsmiths College

University of London

New Cross

London SE14 6NW

We offer full and part-time MPhil and PhD

MA English Local and Regional History

MA History of Art

MRes History

Three new Masters' degrees

MA Cultural History

MA Philosophy and Religion

MA Contemporary Thought and Culture

The Department also offers an MA
tailor made to suit individual needs

Tel: 0171 919 7490

Fax: 0171 919 7398

E-mail: a.peters@gold.ac.uk

or visit our Website at http://www.gold.ac.uk

new formations

new formations has established
a reputation nationally and
internationally as Britain's
most significant interdisciplinary journal of culture, politics
and theory.

Always at the forefront of intellectual debate, *new formations*
has covered issues ranging
from the seduction of perversity to questions of nationalism
and post-colonialism.

'*new formations* is essential
reading for those who want to
understand politics in the light
of the most important trends of
contemporary theory' Chantal
Mouffe

Future Issues are:
new formations no.33
Frontlines/Backyards;
new formations no.34
Dreaming Theory

**SPECIAL OFFER
get new formations no.32
Legal Fictions for
JUST £12.00 POSTFREE
(rrp 14.99)**
Send cheque or money order to
Lawrence & Wishart, address
right.

new formations

LEGAL FICTIONS

A JOURNAL OF CULTURE THEORY POLITICS
NUMBER 32 AUTUMN/WINTER 1997

Or, Why Not Subscribe?

New Formations is published three times a
year. Make sure of your copy by subscribing.

SUBSCRIPTION RATES FOR 1997/98 (3 ISSUES)

Individual Subscriptions
UK   £35.00
Rest of World £38.00

Institutional Subscriptions
UK   £70.00
Rest of World £75.00

Please send one year's subscription
starting with Issue Number _____

I enclose payment of _____
Please send me _____ copies of back issue no. _____
I enclose total payment of _____
Name _____
Address _____
_____ Postcode _____

**Please return this form with cheque or money order (sterling only)
payable to *Lawrence & Wishart* and send to:
Lawrence and Wishart, 99a Wallis Road, London E9 5LN**

depuis 1972

since 1972

art press

revue mensuelle d'art contemporain
contemporary art magazine in English and French, every month

L'ART D'AUJOURD'HUI, LA MÉMOIRE DE DEMAIN
ART HISTORY IN THE MAKING

art press

232

FÉVRIER 98
40 FF US$ 7 295 FB 12,50 FS 6,20 £

Walter Niedermayr Joachim Koester Henrik Plenge Jakobsen Sylvie Fanchon
Photographie allemande : un monde sans pitié / *Harsh New World*
Danse : la peau et les autres lisières / *Borders, Skin, Nudity*
Littérature : Vélimir Khlebnikov, poète futurien / *The Futurian Poet*

L 9240 - 232 - 40,00 F

Dossier Scandinavie

English edition

8, rue François-Villon - 75015 Paris - Tél. : 33 (0)1 53 68 65 65 - Fax : 33 (0)1 53 68 65 85

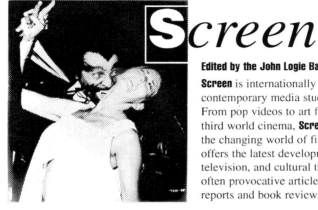

PHILOSOPHY

Radical

88 March/April 1998 £3.95/$7.00

Bruce Robbins	Science-Envy
Chris Thornhill	Negative Theology of Time
Ian Birchall	Heidegger, Audry & Sartre
Andrew Collier	Mind, Reality and Politics
Peter Osborne	Benjamin: Beyond Philosophy

Jonathan Rée on Philosophy in the 17th Century
Lois McNay on Reagan and Kearney on Ricoeur
David Macey on Surrealism

87 Jan/Feb 1998

Roger Harris	The Massification of Higher Education
Lorraine Code	Feminism and Pragmatism
Stella Sandford	Levinas and the Phenomenology of Eros
Jonathan Rée	Rorty's Nation
Michael Löwy	Guy Debord and Romantic Anti-Capitalism

Kathleen Lennon on the Philosophy of Mind
Diana Coole on recent books on Nietzsche
Jean-Jacques Lecercle on Butler's *Excitable Speech*
Sheila Rowbotham on *Beyond Identity Politics*

Subscriptions

individuals: (6 issues) UK £21 Europe £25 ROW surface £27/$44 airmail £33/$54
(12 issues) UK £37 Europe £45 ROW surface £49/$80 airmail £61/$100
institutions: (6 issues) UK £44 Europe £48 ROW surface £50/$82 airmail £55/$91
Cheques payable to *Radical Philosophy Ltd*
Central Books (RP Subs), 99 Wallis Road, London E9 5LN
rp@centralbooks.com   http://www.ukc.ac.uk/secl/philosophy/rp/

parallax

is a cultural studies journal which seeks to initiate alternative forms of cultural theory and criticisms through a critical engagement with the production of cultural knowledges. **parallax** will be of interest to those working in many areas including critical theory, cultural history, gender studies, philosophy, queer theory, english and comparative literature, post colonial theory, art history and of course, cultural studies.

Editors Joanne Morra & Marquard Smith, *Centre for Cultural Studies, University of Leeds, UK*

from tel quel to l'infini

includes **Stephen Bann** on Marcelin Pleynet, **Patrick ffrench** on terror, **Philippe Forest** on Tel Quel and L'Infini, **Suzanne Guerlac** on transgression and the dream of theory, **Jacques Henric** on stories of liberation, **Simeon Hunter** on faultlines and **Julia Kristeva** on the Samuraïs 'tels quels'

kojeve's paris . now bataille

includes **Dennis Hollier, Alphonso Lingis, David Macey, Allan Stoekl,** and **Stanley Rosen** on Alexandre Kojeve and **Carolyn Bailey Gill, Patrick ffrench, Sue Golding, Fred Botting,** and **Scott Wilson** on Georges Bataille

translating 'algeria'

includes **Emily Apter** on "Untranslatable" Algeria, **Hélène Cixous** on her Algeria, **Jacques Derrida** on taking a stand for Algeria, **Assia Djebar** on the burial of Kateb Yacine, **David Macey** on the Algerian with a knife, and **Winnie Woodhull** on colonial conquest and the cinematic femme fatale

work/space

includes **Catherine Greenblatt** on the work of space, **Molly Blieden** on dreaming a paperless office, **Malcolm Miles** on another hero? Public art and the gendered city, **Heide Solbrig** on digital domestics: race, agency, corporate software, and **Stepanie Ellis** on the scope of work/space: uneasy classifications

ORDER FORM

Volume 4 (1998)
Quarterly
ISSN 1353-4645
Institutional: US$198 / £120
Personal: US$58 / £35

Name:_____
Address:_____
_____

I enclose a cheque/postal order/international money order payable to **Taylor & Francis Ltd.**
Please complete and return to Taylor & Francis Ltd, Rankine Rd, Basingstoke, RG24 8PR, UK

Index

contemporary art and culture

depiction
mimesis
replicas
resemblance
repetition
replay
1. 98 rerepresentation
reproduction
copies
multiples
twins
Doppelgänger

P.O Box 151 52, S-104 65 Stockholm, Sweden
tel: +46 8 641 62 96 fax: +46 8 641 96 08 e-mail: magazine.index@mbox200.swipnet.se

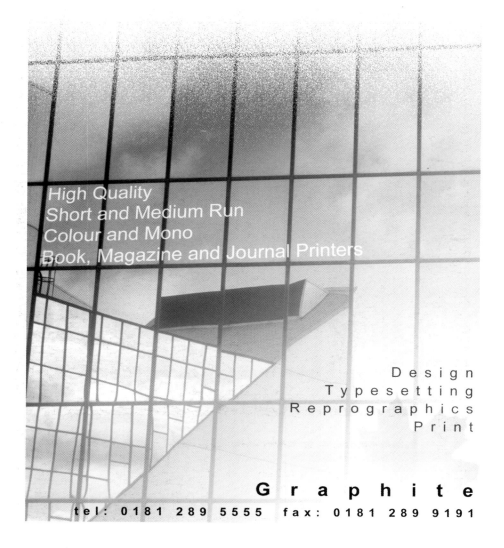

High Quality
Short and Medium Run
Colour and Mono
Book, Magazine and Journal Printers

Design
Typesetting
Reprographics
Print

Graphite

tel: 0181 289 5555   fax: 0181 289 9191

de-, dis-, ex-.

workspace

design for
print
and
internet

t/f: 0171 241 2725
e: workspace@ndirect.co.uk
p: 12 Buttermere Walk
London e8 3ta

Acknowledgments

Our deepest thanks go to those who have generously contributed texts and projects to this volume. Our thanks also go to those whose work did not appear on this occasion: Raymond Bellour, Martin Creed, Daniel Liebeskind, Mark Pimlott.

We acknowledge the following sources where texts have previously appeared: Rosalind Krauss, *A + U* no. 1, 1980; Louis Martin, *assemblage* 11, 1989; Beatriz Colomina, *The Work of Charles and Ray Eames*, edited by Diane Murphy, Harry Abrams, 1997.

We would like to thank the following: Raymonde Coudert, Juliet Cezzar (Eisenman Architects), Tim Clifford (Jon Weber Gallery), Nathalie Defert, Solange Defert, Simon Goodwin, Nancy Holt, Tamara Horbacka, Alan Kipping, Duncan McCorquadale, Metro Pictures Gallery, Steve Newbold, Isabelle Plichon (Musée du Louvre), Sue Rose, Clifton Steinberg.

Copy Editing: Maria Wilson
Printed by: Graphite Inc Ltd.
Design and layout by workspace

de-, dis-, ex-.